INSIDE HAMMER

INSIDE HAMMER

Jimmy Sangster

Reynolds & Hearn Ltd
LONDON

For Toby and Ollie

Title page illustration by Ricky Thaxter.

FRONTISPIECE: *Christopher Lee threatens Melissa Stribling in* **Dracula** *(1958).*

First published in 2001 by
Reynolds & Hearn Ltd
61a Priory Road
Kew Gardens
Richmond
Surrey TW9 3DH

A CIP catalogue record for this book is available from the British Library.

ISBN 1 903111 20 X

Designed by Peri Godbold.

Printed and bound in Great Britain by Biddles Ltd, Guildford, Surrey.

CONTENTS

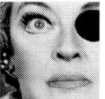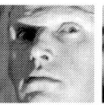

ACKNOWLEDGMENTS

I am indebted to Adrian Rigelsford, Joe McIntyre and Peter Nicholson for the loan of rare stills. Special thanks to Don Fearney, for his invaluable picture research, and Hammer Film Productions, for the provision of items from their archive.

Thanks must go to Wayne Kinsey and his magazine series *The House that Hammer Built*. From these works I was reminded of so much I had forgotten and informed of so much I'd never even known.

Then to Tom Johnson and Deborah Del Vecchio for their books on Hammer, particularly their *Exhaustive Filmography*. Truly exhaustive, truly invaluable.

Also, many thanks to Denis Meikle for his great book on Hammer, *A History of Horrors*, which charts the rise and fall of Hammer. A true horror story. Thanks also to Denis for the generous loan of the *Disciple of Dracula* script.

Thanks, too, to Marcus Hearn and Alan Barnes for *The Hammer Story*, and to Renée Glynne, Mark A Miller, Sue and Colin Cowie, Jonathan Rigby and Gary and Sue Svehla.

With the help of these people this book has been a pleasure to write. Without it, it would have been impossible.

FOREWORD

When my old friend Jimmy Sangster asked me to write the foreword to his book, I looked back to the many happy days we spent at Bray Studios when we were both employed by Hammer Films.

We first worked together in 1962 when I directed a film called *Paranoiac*, which starred Oliver Reed and Janette Scott. Following this we made *Nightmare*, which starred Jennie Linden, and then, even later, *Hysteria* with Hollywood's Robert Webber and Lelia Goldoni. Jimmy wrote the screenplays for all three, and produced the latter two. These were all 'psychological thrillers' and the twists and turns of the plots were prime examples of Jimmy's fertile writing. They were not straight-out 'horror' stories featuring Frankenstein and Dracula, although Jimmy excelled at writing these as well.

What I remember most about working with Jimmy is that although we were shooting horror and fright, our collaboration was always full of laughs and a lot of fun... qualities which still continue in our lasting friendship.

This book, I think, captures those days so well.

Freddie Francis
London,
September 2001

Jimmy Sangster and Freddie Francis reunited at the Festival of Fantastic Films in 1999. Photo: Uwe Sommerlad.

PROLOGUE

One of the main problems of old age is... is... wait a minute... hang in there for a second... right, got it! One of the main problems of old age is the loss of short term memory. I'm not exaggerating, it's as bad as that. Like walking into a room and wondering what the hell you came in for. Or going out of the house and getting a hundred yards down the street and suddenly saying 'Shit, I've left the keys at home' when you just locked the door behind you less than a minute ago. Or patting your pocket to check you've got your wallet at least half a dozen times in five minutes. Or... or... I could go on, but I've forgotten.

But that's short term memory. The long term isn't quite as bad. I can remember 30 years ago like it was last week. Last week I can't remember at all. So, considering that the last time I worked for Hammer was over 25 years ago, I'll probably be able to remember most of the stuff I hope to put in this book. If I can't, I'm sure there'll be people who'll be able to jog my memory. One thing's for sure; if I make a mistake, there's going to be a lot of good folk around who'll be happy to point to the egg on my face.

Because you people out there really do remember. I've had conversations with fans where they ask me a question about a certain movie and I tell them I don't know the answer because the movie was nothing to do with me. Oh yes it was, they reply. You were friendly with Tony Hinds or Michael Carreras and he/they asked you to rewrite a sequence or a couple of scenes for whatever reason. And I still don't remember. Then they pull out some old newspaper

cutting proving they're right and I'm some forgetful old codger who, maybe, shouldn't be allowed out on his own. And, even more amazing, some of these people weren't even born when these movies were made.

So why have they lasted? (The movies, not the people.) Why do I get invited to Hammer film festivals? Why do they *have* Hammer film festivals? A celebration of a couple of dozen movies, most of them made over 30 years ago, some close to 50 years ago. A rhetorical question, I'm afraid.

I was recently reminded yet again of the the perils of senility when an American company asked me to provide a running commentary over the DVDs of three of the movies I directed. Correction... not a running commentary, more a running reminiscence. While the movie was on, I answered questions about my career with Hammer, put to me by Marcus Hearn. Or rather I tried to answer questions. Most of the time I needed considerable prompting by Marcus. So, when he suggested I write this book I thought he must be crazy. But he did, and I agreed, provided he jogged my memory from time to time.

So what have I written about? The Gothics are obviously the films which everybody is most interested in. Trouble is, with the Gothics I was only the writer. I was not employed on the production side at all. That came later when I started writing my 'psycho' type movies. That's when I got to produce and eventually direct. More of which later.

Sure, I was involved with Hammer before the Gothics, but I suspect that is only of passing interest too. But the title of this book is *Inside Hammer*. And that's what you're going to get. Remember, the

Gothics were just a section of Hammer's work. The most important section, I admit. It's what put them on the map. But there was a lot more, before, during and after. And, while I tried to keep it short, like it or not, I started at the beginning. And it's no good trying to contact me if you want your money back. According to the Writers' Guild of Great Britain, I'm long gone. I quote from a letter they sent to Mark Miller, the author of a first-rate book on Peter Cushing and Christopher Lee. He wanted to get hold of me, ask me a few questions for his book. So he wrote to the WGGB asking for my address. They replied, in a letter dated 25 September 1989:

Dear Mr Miller,
Thank you for your letter of 18th September 1989. Jimmy Sangster is now deceased.

So read and, hopefully, enjoy this book from beyond the grave. I certainly enjoyed writing it... almost as much as I enjoyed doing what I have written about those many years gone by. Because they were good years. Great years, in fact. I'm sure some of the bad memories will come creeping back once I get into my stride, because somewhere back there during the last 50 years there must have been a couple of bad days. But for the life of me, I can't recall them right now.

*The Hammer crew during production of **The Saint's Return** early in 1953. Seated left to right: designer J Elder Wills, Jimmy, production manager John F 'Pinky' Green, clapper boy Tommy Friswell, director Seymour Friedman, producer Anthony Hinds, cinematographer Jimmy Harvey, continuity supervisor Renée Glynne, electrician Jack Curtis and make-up man Phil Leakey (kneeling). Camera operator Len Harris is between Hinds and Harvey.*

CHAPTER 1

The Exclusive Years

I am acting under the assumption that most of you have not read my autobiography, *Do You Want it Good or Tuesday*, published in 1997. If you have, I thank you profusely, especially if you bought rather than borrowed it. But you're going to have to bear with me because there's going to be a lot of repetition. One can hardly write about a period of one's life in one book and then write about the same period in another book without there being a strong similarity. But this book is about my experience, my life if you like, with Hammer and there's a whole pile of stuff in it that I didn't write about in the first book. So, if you're standing in the bookshop reading this, go ahead, buy it. I promise you, you won't be wasting your money.

I first started working for Hammer, or Exclusive Films as it was then known, on their tenth or eleventh movie. They'd made five before the second world war, including one (*The Mystery of the Mary Celeste*) which starred Bela Lugosi. A little incongruous that the only movie made for the great horror film company, Hammer, by the great horror film star, Bela Lugosi, was not, in the true sense, a horror film. But all that was long before my time. After the war Exclusive/Hammer made seven movies before I joined them.

My arrival at Hammer was due to the fact that I was working on a movie produced by a man named Mario Zampi, who was commissioned by Hammer to produce *Dick Barton Strikes Back*. Dick Barton was a poor man's James Bond, a very poor man's. But Hammer had made a couple of Barton pictures earlier and they'd done quite well at the box office. So they decided they'd do number three. Zampi was supposed to bring his

entire crew over to Hammer to make the movie, but he absconded a couple of weeks before it was due to start. Whether he took any of the money with him, I have no idea, but suddenly the movie was left rudderless.

So in stepped Anthony Hinds, the son of Will Hammer, to take over. It was his first movie, my first Hammer movie, and, if memory serves me, the first movie, too, for Michael Carreras, the son of James Carreras, although both of them had worked for the distribution part of the company prior to this. Michael and I had recently done our National Service stint, something we all had to do back then, me in the Royal Air Force, Michael in one of the Guard's regiments. Neither of us advanced very far, both of us considering the whole affair a complete waste of our time. After all, the war was over for God's sake! Let's get on with our lives.

*Bela Lugosi starred in one of Hammer's earliest productions, **The Mystery of the Mary Celeste** (1936), renamed **Phantom Ship** in the USA.*

ANTHONY HINDS

The son of William Hinds (aka Will Hammer), Tony was the big boss as far as I was concerned. Although James Carreras ran the company, one rarely came into contact with him and Michael Carreras was always more of a mate than a boss even if he was that too. I remember Tony mostly as an extremely nice man and very funny. I also remember him as the man who gave me my first chance as assistant director, production manager and eventually writer. Unlike other producers I've known, and there are a lot of them, Tony was non-aggressive and non-confrontational which made him a joy to work for. He eventually became fed up with the job, mainly, I think, because of the politics which seemed to play a larger and larger part in the company's affairs. He was a good producer, a good writer and it was a great pity when he finally gave it all up and went to live in the country... from where, incidentally, he's almost impossible to winkle out.

The movie was shot at Viking studios, a tiny place off Kensington High Street in London. The last time I was there, a few years back, it had been turned into a private house and the owner was throwing a grand party in a marquee on the back lawn. He didn't even believe me when I told him his home used to be a movie studio. We also shot extensive locations in Blackpool. More Dick Barton movies were in the pipeline but Don Stannard, the star, was killed in a car accident while leaving a garden party held by Hammer to celebrate the release of the movie. Also in the car at the time was the actor Sebastian Cabot, who played the villain in this film and then went on to sitcom fame in America. I was in the car behind Don's and watched as it went out of control, off the road, and down a steep hill. I was the only person around a

couple of days later when the police called and asked if I'd identify the body.

The garden party had been held at Dial Close, the first of the country house 'studios' used by Hammer. Four movies were made at Dial Close. Dr Morelle, PC 49, Celia and Meet Simon Cherry. Then some kind of application for planning permission was turned down and the company moved to Oakley Court, where we shot another five. The Man in Black, Room to Let, Someone at the Door, What the Butler Saw and The Lady Craved Excitement.

During this period eyes were fixed on the wreck of a place next door. A large, fairly old house called Down Place. The owners, the Davies family, lived in a small wing of the house while the rest of the place was used to store army surplus duffel coats – 30,000 of them. Unfortunately the roof had sprung a couple of leaks and water had soaked into the piles of duffel coats on the first floor, making them so heavy that they brought the ceilings down. However, Hammer saw the potential of the place and negotiations started. While these negotiations were going on, we moved to Gilston Park for Black Widow, The Rossiter Case, To Have and to Hold and The Dark Light. Then, at last, to Down Place, which was rechristened Bray Studios.

The house that sticks most in the memory was Oakley Court. Any fan of the old Hammer movies will know what it looks like both inside and out. We rented the place furnished and weren't allowed to move a stick of it. It was said that you could arrive at a cinema in the middle of a movie and know it was a Hammer film because you'd seen the same set, furnished the same way, in their last three pictures. Only the actors were different. And such was the repertory-type casting that Hammer favoured, even they were difficult to distinguish from one movie to the next. Michael Medwin, Hy Hazell, Jean Lodge, Sid James, Anthony Forwood... there's a bunch of names to pull them in at the box office.

One of the joys of working at the places before Bray Studios was the fact that many of us 'lived in'. The houses were all large, all fully furnished, so we had our own bedrooms and Hammer would employ a couple to look after us and cook our breakfast and dinner. I imagine they must have charged us something for this, but whatever it was, it was a deal.

Sometime during the shooting of these movies I made it to first assistant director thanks mainly to Tony Hinds, who took a chance on me at age 22. He thought long and hard about this. It was a ball-breaking job if you're making as many pictures as Hammer were then. You have to run a shooting unit at the same time as you're preparing the next picture, due on the floor two weeks after the current one finishes. The minimum wage for a first assistant director, as laid down by the ACTT union, was £16 per week. In a fit of generosity, Tony signed me on at £20 per week to include overtime. Good move on his part, bad on mine considering the amount of overtime I worked. But hell, who cared? My yearly salary had reached four figures.

It was also during this period that I met and married my first wife, Monica, who was hairdresser on many of the movies. I didn't even like her when we first met. It was my job in the winter to lay and light a coal fire in the make-up room and in the hairdresser's room, if required. Phil Leakey, the make-up man back then, never wanted a fire. Monica *always* wanted one.

Eventually, when we moved to Bray, the 'living in' came to an end. There was no furniture and every room, large and small, was put to studio use. Hammer would run a coach from Hammersmith Broadway to the studios every morning. The coach left at 7.30 on the dot and tough luck anybody who didn't make it. We'd stop for a very quick breakfast break in Windsor and be in the studio, on set, by 8.30 am. Try to do that in today's traffic even with the M4 motorway, which didn't exist back then.

Monday, Tuesday and Thursday we worked until six pm, Wednesday and Friday until 5.30. The unions were very strong in those days. We had the ACT which covered camera crew, sound and production staff, NATKE which covered the hairdressers, wardrobe staff and make-up, along with the chippies, painters and plasterers, and the ETU, the electricians' trade union. There was also Equity, which covered actors, and a fifth union I can't even remember which was supposed to take care of crowd players. And all these unions were as tough as old boots. They'd worked hard for their agreements and, by Christ, we'd better stick to them. As assistant director, I was supposed to call an end to the day's shooting at ten minutes before knocking off time. This was supposed to be so everybody could wash their hands, take a pee and tidy up before going home. What it in fact meant was that three minutes after my calling 'wrap' everybody was on the coach clamouring for it to get going.

However, such was the atmosphere at Hammer in those days that I, as assistant director, could 'borrow' time. In other words, I'd go, say, five minutes over for the director to complete a particular shot and before I yelled 'wrap' I'd thank the crew and tell them I owed them five minutes the next day. No other studio, anywhere, could have got away with this. It was part of the 'repertory company' atmosphere that Hammer developed in those days. The staff trusted the management not to screw them. And the management didn't.

Oakley Court, situated between Maidenhead and Bray, was briefly used as a studio by Hammer during the late forties and early fifties.

Down Place was renamed Bray Studios, and played host to numerous Hammer productions in the fifties and sixties. Jimmy was production manager on **Dick Turpin – Highwayman**, a colour short produced at the studio in October 1955.

They even brought in a bonus system which was paid to certain crew members if the movie finished on schedule. And boy, did we churn out the movies, going straight from one to the next with only a two or three week break between them.

The crew became semi-permanent. Frank Searle, a thoroughly competent director. Jimmy Harvey, lighting cameraman. Len Harris, camera operator. Harry Oakes, his focus puller. Percy Britten, boom man. Renée Glynne, continuity. Jimmy Needs, supervising editor. And those old faithfuls who were mainly responsible for persuading Tony Hinds to promote me to first assistant, namely Jack Curtis, chief electrician, Tommy Money, property master, and dear old Arthur Barnes, the production manager. Without those three, who told Tony they'd make sure I didn't fall flat on my arse, who knows how long it would have taken me to get the promotion.

And in all this, nothing particular stands out in my memory... Stanley Baker playing a milkman with one line in *The Rossiter Case*; Harry Fine, later to be producer on *Lust for a Vampire*, playing a small part in

*F*IRST *Assistant Jimmy Sangster appears to be having trouble during the shooting of Exclusive's " The Black Widow," due for release October 22. With him in this picture are, left to right: Peter Bryan (Camera operator); Jimmy Sangster (first assistant); Jimmy Harvey (lighting cameraman); with stars Jennifer Jayne and Robert Ayres.*

A bad hair day for first assistant Jimmy Sangster during production of **The Black Widow** in April 1950.

To Have and To Hold; Sidney James in at least four early Hammers, usually playing a villain.

Then Hammer signed a deal with an American producer who was to provide us with an American 'star' for future pictures. The first was Robert Preston, who, up to then, had never been a star, rather an extremely competent and recognisable second lead, the guy who never got the gal. Only later did he become a big star in *The Music Man* and *Victor Victoria* among others. One would like to think it was because of the Hammer picture he did (*Cloudburst*) but, trust me, it wasn't.

After him we had Richard Carlson, playing a private eye in a movie called *Whispering Smith Hits London*. I remember him mainly because Michael Carreras and I went to his hotel the day he was packing to leave after completing his part in the movie. His wife had obviously done a lot of shopping while they were in London and he couldn't get all their stuff into the suitcases. So he gave Michael and I one each of his suits. Real American suits... cool, man!

Then came George Brent and Marguerite Chapman, a couple of fast-fading Hollywood legends in *The Last Page*. A supporting part in this one was played by Diana Dors. And very good she was, too. In America they changed the title to *Man Bait* and billed Diana above the title, with poor old George as co-star beneath the title and Marguerite Chapman nowhere to be seen at all. The film is of passing interest to some because it was the first time Terry Fisher directed a film for Hammer. Come to think of it, he didn't do a very good job.

Then came *Wings of Danger*. This one starred Zachary Scott from Hollywood, along with the gorgeous Kay Kendall, and introduced to the screen the sexy Diane Cilento.

Then there was *Stolen Face*. This starred Paul Henreid, the suave mid-European who had become famous for lighting two cigarettes with Bette Davis. It also starred Lizabeth Scott, a very sexy Hollywood actress who astounded me on the first day of shooting by telling me she wouldn't be available Wednesday or Thursday because she was due for a period. I remember asking her 'A period what?' I was very naïve in those days.

This movie also marked Hammer moving out of Bray for the first time. The interiors were all shot at

Wings of Danger *was partly filmed on location in Rye during September 1951. Jimmy (far right) chances his arm with a slot machine, Renée Glynne (far left) looks on and American leading man Zachary Scott samples the local ale with one of the regulars.*

Riverside Studios. The only other point of interest in the making of this movie was that Edith Head, three times an Oscar winner for costume design, did Lizabeth Scott's wardrobe. This, I hasten to say, was as a favour to Lizabeth, because Hammer certainly wasn't going to pay the kind of money Edith earned.

Then, for reasons I don't know, Hammer slowed down and finally stopped production altogether. That's it, says I. The movie business in England is finished, let's try pastures new. Monica and I packed our bags and emigrated to Canada where we lasted about six months before borrowing enough money to return to England. Almost immediately I got a call from Tony Hinds. Would I like my old job back? I found out later that he wanted somebody else but the guy wasn't available, and he acted under the assumption that the devil you know is better than the one you don't.

So back to work on a movie called *The Flanagan Boy*, starring the very sexy Barbara Payton, her second movie for Hammer. Then came Hammer's first venture into outer space, *Spaceways*, with Howard Duff and Eva Bartok. They needn't have bothered. It was pretty dire, mainly due to the budget restrictions. These days they spend more money on ten seconds of special effects than Hammer spent on the entire movie. Terry Fisher

directed it with his customary good humour, but by now he was getting a little bored with the stuff he was being asked to do and it was beginning to show.

The next movie was *The Saint's Return*. This was years before the first Saint TV series although a couple of movies had been made in Hollywood with George Sanders playing the Saint. This time it was Louis Hayward, an actor who, if one was to believe the director the Americans sent with him, had been a pretty big deal in Hollywood. I know this because the director in question, Seymour Friedman, raised all kinds of problems about the size of Hayward's dressing room, the size of the make-up room and where was Mr Hayward going to take a pee because he was certainly too big a star to pee with the peasants. I, being one of the peasants he was referring to, wasn't very impressed. But Louis Hayward turned out to be a very polite, reasonably talented, nice guy.

Much later, and nothing to do with Hammer, Seymour Friedman became vice-president of business affairs for Columbia TV in Hollywood and was partly responsible for me getting my first job over there. So he couldn't have been all that pissed off with me during the shooting of *The Saint's Return*. Diana Dors was in this one too. By now she was referring to herself as 'the

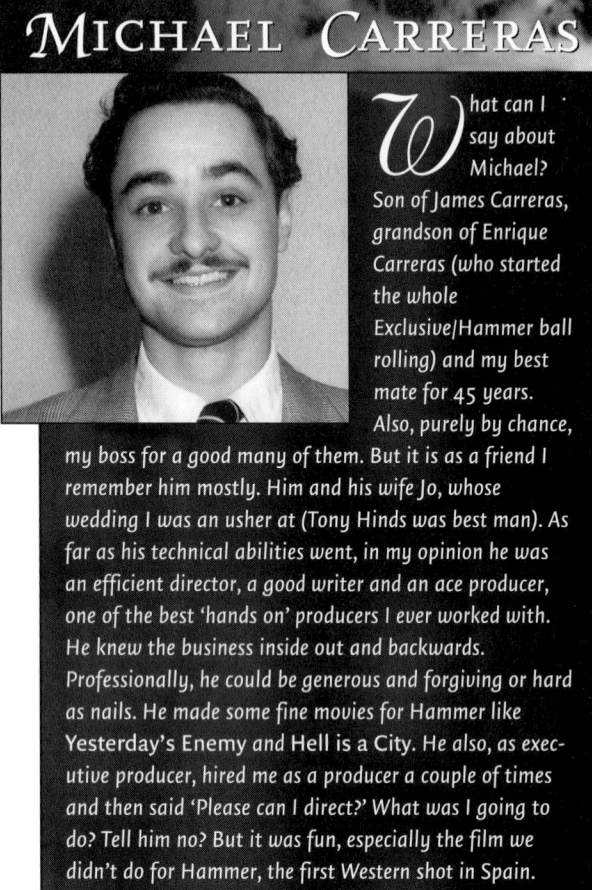

MICHAEL CARRERAS

*W*hat can I say about Michael? Son of James Carreras, grandson of Enrique Carreras (who started the whole Exclusive/Hammer ball rolling) and my best mate for 45 years. Also, purely by chance, my boss for a good many of them. But it is as a friend I remember him mostly. Him and his wife Jo, whose wedding I was an usher at (Tony Hinds was best man). As far as his technical abilities went, in my opinion he was an efficient director, a good writer and an ace producer, one of the best 'hands on' producers I ever worked with. He knew the business inside out and backwards. Professionally, he could be generous and forgiving or hard as nails. He made some fine movies for Hammer like Yesterday's Enemy and Hell is a City. He also, as exec- utive producer, hired me as a producer a couple of times and then said 'Please can I direct?' What was I going to do? Tell him no? But it was fun, especially the film we didn't do for Hammer, the first Western shot in Spain. Dear Michael. I miss him a great deal.

only sex symbol Britain has produced since Lady Godiva'. She could have been right. She was a fun lady and never really took the 'sex symbol' side of her career too seriously. As for the shooting of the movie, I remember we shot in mid-winter, the weather was foul, we went way over schedule and wound up with a fairly boring picture.

Terry Fisher came aboard for the next film, *Blood Orange*. This one starred Tom Conway, whose main claim to fame was that he was George Sanders' brother. According to *Today's Cinema*, 'the most valu- able aspect of the picture' was Jimmy Harvey's camera- work and J Elder Wills' art direction.

This was followed by *36 Hours*, an unmemorable movie starring Dan Duryea. I was looking through the

crew list trying to come up with something interesting to say about somebody... anybody, and the only thing that stood out was the fact that it was practically the same crew that worked on the ten previous pictures.

Talk about names from the past. There's Jimmy Harvey who, as cameraman, was the assistant director's (me) delight. He was quick, efficient, and never asked for a retake. Whereas his predecessor a few movies back, Cedric Williams, while turning out very reasonable-looking movies, took too long to light the scenes in the first place, and then was quite capable of deciding after take two or three that he wanted to change the lights. Then there was Bill Salter, the sound man. A real Victor Meldrew was Bill, the original grumpy old man. He could hear aeroplanes through his headphones before the bloody things had even taken off from Heathrow, 15 miles away. And he'd interrupt the scene in the middle to tell us about it. As for the movie itself, like I just said, it was just another Hammer movie which trade magazine *Kinematograph Weekly* described as 'adequate'.

The next up was *Face the Music*. This was a pet project of Michael Carreras who produced it because the hero was a trumpet player. Both Michael and I were huge big band jazz fans. It was a fun movie to make. We shot on location at the London Palladium with the Kenny Baker Orchestra on stage, and Kenny himself provided the playback tracks for the trumpeter hero, played by Alex Nicol.

Alex was in the next picture called *The House Across the Lake*. It was shot from a screenplay written by the director Ken Hughes from his own novel. Ken later went on to direct *Casino Royale*, *Chitty Chitty Bang Bang* and a whole bunch of other big time movies. For this one, Hollywood sent us Hillary Brooke to co-star with Alex Nicol.

'Hillary who...? I can hear you saying.

Feel free – most of the crew said the same thing at the time. But the film turned out to be quite good in a B-picture kind of way. Which was okay because B- pictures were what we were making in those days.

The next film I worked on was called *Five Days*. It starred American actor Dane Clark. This was his third picture for Hammer but the first one I worked on with him. A very good actor, but a real pain in the neck to deal with on almost every level. It was indifferently directed by a nice guy, Montgomery Tully, who later went on to direct one of the Hammer comedies, *I Only Arsked!*.

Round about here, the good times stopped. At least, they did for me. I was promoted from assistant director to production manager. So what's he bitching about? I can hear you asking; a promotion; more money; more clout. Let me tell you about assistant directing as opposed to production managing. As assistant director your main responsibility is the efficient running of the set, trying to second guess the director as to what he might want next and making sure it's there when he's ready. You're in the thick of the action, dealing on a one-to-one basis with the whole cast and crew. It's a responsible job, but it's fun. At least it is if you're doing it properly. I loved it.

Okay, so now you have the production manager. You're the guy who runs the organisation of the whole enchillada. The assistant director might run the set, but if it wasn't for the production manager, there wouldn't be a set. If anything goes wrong, anything at all, he gets the blame. If he does his job well and

nothing goes wrong... so big deal! That's what he's being paid for. Say, for example, the shooting requires a week's location in some God-forsaken spot 50 miles from anywhere. The production manager is responsible for finding accommodation for upwards of 70 people, feeding them, getting permission to shoot there, arranging for transport, portable loos, make-up caravans, dressing room trailers, somewhere warm and dry for those 70 people to eat... the list is endless. At least, it seemed that way in my day. Nowadays, on the larger movies, they employ location managers, transport controllers... you name it, there's someone there to deal with it. Makes me wonder sometimes what the production manager does with his spare time.

Anyway, suddenly I was production manager. The movie was a piece called *The Stranger Came Home*, screenplay by Michael Carreras, his first I think, based on a novel by George Sanders. I don't know whether the novel was a success, but the picture certainly wasn't. Indifferently directed by Terry Fisher, it starred Paulette Goddard who, unlike some of the people Hollywood had sent us, had been a real star in her time,

*Camera operator Len Harris (top left) and assistant director Jimmy Sangster (beneath him) with Hollywood import Dan Duryea during production of **36 Hours** at Bray in May 1953.*

Filming **Face the Music** at the London Palladium on 25 June 1953 with bandleader Kenny Baker (far right). Michael Carreras (second left) watches camera operator Len Harris and director Terence Fisher (in glasses). Continuity supervisor Renée Glynne kneels beneath the camera and star Alex Nicol mimes to the trumpet playback.

an Academy Award nominee and an ex-Mrs Charlie Chaplin. She was a polite, ice-cold lady who never complained about anything upfront but who would lay out all her problems to her driver on the way home each night. He'd tell me all about it first thing next day and I'd take care of it without having to discuss it with her. I learned, much later, that she knew the driver was telling me everything and it was her way of getting what she wanted without confrontation. This picture marked the end of her career. She returned to Hollywood and packed it in. It should have marked the end of a couple of other careers too. 'A third rate British who-dun-it' according to the *New York Times*.

Then Lloyd Bridges arrived for *Third Party Risk*. While not exactly a big star, and long before his sons became famous, he was, nevertheless, probably the best value that Robert Lippert, the American side of the business in those days, sent us. He was a very pleasant, affable man. I remember him mainly because I often found him wandering around the studio grounds looking for locations that he felt would open up the picture. As usual, we were on a tight budget, something I was well aware of because I made it out and, in spite of the fact most of the movie was supposed to take place in Spain, we never left the studio. Don't ask me how we did it! A couple of bullfight posters, a mantilla for the leading lady, Maureen Swanson, and rattle some castanets in the score... Olé! Hammer's

version of a foreign location (at least, in those days).

It was during this movie that I worked out that Tony Hinds had a speaker in his office wired up to the mike on the set. My office had a window that overlooked his office and occasionally I would see Tony run out of his office, jump into his car and drive off heaven knows where. When that happened I knew that within a couple of minutes I'd be getting a call from the set to let me know that some form of shit had hit the fan and would I/could I take care of it because nobody could find the producer. I think Tony believed that if he wasn't around the problem wouldn't escalate. Let the production manager deal with it, that's what he was being paid for.

Next came *Mask of Dust*. A Formula One racing movie. America sent us Richard Conte for this one and we did locations at Goodwood race track with cars which might have been okay in their time, but nowadays look like clapped-out wrecks. It was Terry Fisher's eleventh film for Hammer. He was a production manager's dream. If I told him that we had to finish by six pm today because somebody else wanted to use the race track or he had to finish with a certain actor by a certain date, he never kicked up a fuss. 'All right, dear boy,' was his standard response.

But, in spite of the fact we used some pretty impressive racing drivers on this shoot (Stirling Moss, Reg Parnell, John Cooper), it still turned out to be a pretty boring picture. Let's face it, a dozen or so cars tearing around a race track ain't much to watch unless the drama that surrounds the event is gripping enough to make you really interested in who's driving. Richard Landau's script wasn't. As *Variety* said, ' An OK entry for a minor double bill.'

Then Hammer embarked on their first tits-and-swords epics. This early one was bigger on the swords than the tits. They came much later. It was also the first movie they shot in colour. *The Men of Sherwood Forest* was the title. It could as well have been 'Robin Hood Rides Again'. It was yet another version of the old standard. King Richard is prisoner in Europe; his throne is usurped by wicked Prince John and Robin Hood rides to the rescue. Don Taylor starred as Robin. A nice guy who later became a director in Hollywood. He also married Hazel Court, more of whom later.

I know I've been bitching about being a production manager, but this movie ran very smoothly. We shot locations quite close to the studio and the weather was kind to us. Val Guest was one of the most efficient directors I'd ever worked with. Every day, when work started, he'd pin on a board an outline of every shot he intended doing that day. Great for the assistant director who could marshal all the technical crew accordingly. And pretty good for the production manager too.

The cast contained a whole bunch of Hammer regulars like Reginald Beckwith, Harold Lang, John van Eyssen, Leonard Sachs and, way down the line as one of the Merry Men, Bernard Bresslaw. A postscript on this production was that Hammer were later sued by one of the stunt men because he fell off his horse. Needless to say, he lost the case.

Hammer then embarked on a couple of movies that I wasn't involved in because I was preparing *Break in the Circle*. My wife Monica worked as hairdresser on this, one of the few pictures we worked on together after I became production manager and one of the last pictures she worked on for Hammer before she became pregnant.

Forrest Tucker came over from Hollywood for this one and it was directed by Val Guest. It was a ball-breaker of a movie. We had two locations, one in Polperro, a small fishing harbour in Cornwall. One of the guide books describes it as 'a fishing village with

streets so narrow that traffic is banned.' Great for the tourists and the residents, but how the hell was I supposed to get the equipment down to the harbour every day and make sure the crew got fed and watered on time. I don't know, even now, how I arranged it. I guess I must have bribed some of the locals.

Added to that there was the hotel problem. There was one hotel with six rooms. That took care of the producer, the director and the four most important members of the cast. For the other 55 members of cast and crew I had to rent rooms from the locals who knew they were onto a good thing and charged us accordingly. Also, sometime during the making of this movie I had the most flaming row with the associate producer, Mickey Delamar. I was so pissed off I went to Michael Carreras, who was producing, and told him I was going to quit. Dear Michael, he told me not to behave like a prima donna arsehole and get on with my job. Which, needless to say, I did. But I never really made it up with Mickey Delamar, who hung around for a couple more pictures.

The second location on *Break in the Circle* was even worse. Hamburg in Germany. The crew never stopped bitching about the food, the accommodation, the fact they couldn't understand the locals because they all spoke German, the fact we were working them too hard. You name it, they complained. This was my first foreign location. I learned later that it was par for the course. The British film units, in those days, always bitched. I'm sure it's a lot better these days. The unions have lost most of their muscle and they don't try to bully the producer any longer. They also get paid a hell of a lot more money.

Forrest Tucker was our Hollywood star for this one, accompanied by Eva Bartok and Marius Goring. Eva was very sweet, a girl who learned her script word for word including typographical errors. She did the first rehearsal of a scene one day where she was required to shout farewell to some character or another.

'Good fuck!' she yelled.

It took Val Guest five minutes to explain to her it was a misprint.

The next movie I did for Hammer as production manager, and coincidentally the last, was the worst experience of them all. And it wasn't made any easier by the fact that I'd written it.

DONALD WOLFIT
MICHAEL MEDWIN

in

A Man on the Beach

CINEPANORAMA AND EASTMANCOLOUR

CHAPTER 2

A Man on the Beach
X the Unknown

A MAN ON THE BEACH
(filmed 1955, released 1956)

X THE UNKNOWN
(filmed January to February 1956,
released 21 September 1956)

There's not much I can say about my first screenplay credit, *A Man on the Beach*, other than that it was less than 30 minutes long and was directed by the late, great Joe Losey. He was a fugitive from Senator McCarthy and his House Un-American Activities Committee. Unable to get a job in Hollywood, he'd come to England, along with a number of other talented writers and directors, like Carl Foreman, who had written the screenplay for *High Noon*.

There was no way Joe was going to get a decent job over here. The big-time English producers wouldn't touch him or any of the others with a barge pole (although they did later, providing they worked under pseudonyms). So Joe accepted the directing job on *A Man on the Beach*, for which he must have been paid the equivalent of a couple of weeks' rent. And he made a very good job of it, turning an indifferent screenplay based on a short story by Victor Canning into a stylish little piece of screen entertainment.

The story itself was simple almost to the point of banality. A guy, dressed as an old woman, robs a casino in France. He has a falling out with his co-conspirator who is also acting as his driver. They fight and our 'hero' gets wounded. But he manages to overpower the accomplice, stick him in the car and send it over the cliff into the sea. Bloodied, he staggers to a small house

on the beach where he encounters the occupant, a dour old guy who patches up his wound. He decides he's going to have to kill the old guy before he leaves so he won't be able to identify him, only, at the last moment, to discover the old guy's blind. Big denouement.

Like I said, the picture was better than the story. What kind of release it had, I can't imagine. But Hammer made quite a few short subjects around that time. *Dick Turpin – Highwayman*, on which I served as production manager, and half a dozen others. They were all well made with good, solid casts.

Back to *A Man on the Beach*. It starred Donald Wolfit, a grand old man of the theatre later caricatured in the play and subsequent movie *The Dresser*, along with Michael Medwin, a Hammer stalwart, and the most regular Hammer player of them all, Michael Ripper. Most times I forget all about this movie. When asked what my first screenplay was I invariably say *X the Unknown*. In fact, I wrote one little piece before either of them, another short subject which I entitled *The Camera*. Tony Hinds read it, said it was okay, but he didn't want to make it. But it probably took that to convince him it was okay to hire me to write *A Man on the Beach*. Which he did. Which I did. Which Joe Losey did and which I imagine cost practically no money at all in spite of a location in France. While I was still employed on a semi-permanent basis by Hammer, I had nothing to do with the actual shooting of the movie because I was too busy writing *X the Unknown*.

So how come a company like Hammer entrusted the writing of a full-length feature film to a production manager with virtually no writing experience? It happened like this. *The Quatermass Xperiment* had just gone into release and rather taken everyone by

CLASSIC SCENE

A MAN ON THE BEACH

*T*he Rolls-Royce going off the cliff, supposedly carrying Michael Ripper with it. I wasn't on the location, so I don't know how they did it or with what, and there's nobody around to ask any more. But I'm sure they didn't wreck that lovely vintage Rolls that was used in the earlier scenes. Except, knowing Joe Losey, as I eventually did, maybe they did and he got away with it with an 'Oops... I'm sorry.'

  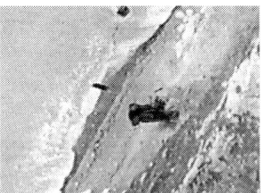 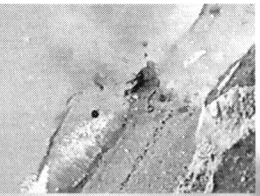

surprise. While everyone hoped it would make good money, this was ridiculous. It was coining it. Deservedly so, as it happens. Based on Nigel Kneale's successful TV series it had a pre-sold audience, but it would have made it anyway. It was a good movie, very ably directed by Val Guest.

Come to think of it, I had a hand in the shooting, a very small hand admittedly, but I was there. Those of you who saw the movie will remember that the plot required huge amounts of electricity to be redirected to a scaffolding inside Westminster Abbey where the multi-tentacled monster had taken refuge and was growing apace. They needed shots of London landmarks being blacked out as the electricity supply is diverted. One of these landmarks was Battersea Power Station. In those days it wasn't the empty, roofless shell it is now, it was a provider of electricity for a good part of London on the south side of the river. I guess Val Guest and the main unit were off shooting somewhere else, either that, or they didn't want to involve a large unit in a night location. So there was just me and a three-man camera team.

I arranged with the guy in charge of the power station that he would switch off the floodlights at exactly midnight while we photographed it from the other side of the river. We synchronised our watches, I gave him a £25 backhander and joined the crew where we had set up the camera. At 30 seconds to midnight we rolled the camera and, exactly on time, the floodlights illuminating the power station went out. I was about to tell the guys to cut the camera and let's go home when other lights started to go out along the river frontage. Obviously I'd overtipped the guy. He blacked out a huge part of London south of the river and didn't switch the power on again until 15 minutes later. There was a short paragraph about the affair in the newspapers the next day. 'Mysterious blackout south of the river'.

But I'm digressing. I'm supposed to be writing about *X the Unknown* and how I came to write the screenplay. James Carreras, more of whom later, desperately wanted a follow-up to *Quatermass*, a science fiction movie which could be made quickly and, as was his wont, cheaply. Trouble was, there wasn't anything around. Tony Hinds, Michael Carreras and myself were sitting around the office one day congratulating ourselves at how well *Quatermass* was doing at the box office and where should we go for lunch when I came up with the idea that, whereas in all the science fiction stories I'd read to date, the monster or the threat always comes from outer space...

'How about one that comes from inner space... the middle of the earth? Cheaper to dig a hole than construct a rocket ship.'

'What happens next?' Tony wanted to know.

'Don't ask me,' said I. 'I'm not a writer. Unless... maybe... this scientist...'

'Better if he...' said Tony.

'How about if...' said Michael.

We never did get to go to lunch that day. We sent out for sandwiches and in about an hour we'd knocked out the bare bones of a story. All we needed now was somebody to write the treatment and the screenplay. This being Hammer, nobody wanted to invest any hard cash in the project at this stage so Tony suggested I have a go at it.

'I'm a production manager, not a writer,' says I.

'You wrote *A Man on the Beach*,' says Tony.

I figured that was short and didn't count.

Michael suggested that maybe I'd turn out to be a better writer than production manager because I certainly wasn't very good at that.

'Go and write it,' said Tony. 'If we like it, then we'll pay you. If we don't, we won't.'

After I made sure I would still be getting my production manager salary, I told them I'd have a go. I borrowed a typewriter from my secretary and went to work on the treatment. For some writers the treatment is just an extended storyline, to others it's a detailed blueprint of what the script is going to turn out to be. I belong to the latter school. My treatments can run to 50 or 60 pages. Everything save the dialogue. I worked very hard on this, my first treatment, and I enjoyed myself immensely. The idea that one could make a living doing something that was so enjoyable seemed, at the time, almost ludicrous. I say 'at the time' but, in retrospect, its something that has never changed. I've been one of those incredibly lucky people who has made a good living all his life, doing what he likes best.

I duly handed in the treatment. Tony liked it and offered me the same deal.

'Go and write the script. If we like it we'll pay you. If we don't, we won't.'

As far as I was concerned, with the treatment, the hard work had been done. The characters had been defined, the scenes blocked and, most important, the overall construction of the piece had been laid out. In my opinion, this is the most important aspect of any screenplay. Act one, act two, act three. A beginning, a middle and an end. It's the foundation of the whole thing. Without it, there's no way you're going to get a decent screenplay. Dialogue comes way down the line. Everybody's going to mess with the dialogue, the director, the producer and the actors. Whereas, if the basic construction is good, it can't be messed with without bringing down the whole thing. With *X the Unknown*, I guess I got lucky. I got it right first time. I delivered the shooting script and hey! They liked it. I got paid a pittance but all of a sudden I was a fully fledged screenwriter.

There's a line in the movie – 'Let's not conjure up visions of nameless horrors creeping about in the night' – which is exactly what I set out to do. Conjure up nameless horrors. Put a lot of people into terrible danger, especially helpless people, innocent little children, maybe throw in a couple of cuddly pets. Then make sure none of them actually get hurt. The story was simple, almost formulaic. A mass of sludge emerges from the centre of the earth, greedy for any radioactive material on which to feed itself. It flows around the countryside causing chaos, havoc and death wherever it goes. Its climactic venture is to an atomic energy centre where our hero, the absent-minded professor, works. There it gorges itself on enough energy to fuel half-a-dozen nuclear bombs before retreating back to its hole in the ground. It's got to be destroyed before it re-emerges. And that's what happens. A simple, straightforward storyline with a well-defined beginning, middle and end.

I watched it on video the other day. It's a pretty good movie. The critics liked it. 'Gripping science fiction... good, grisly fun... vastly entertaining.' That's the one I liked, 'vastly entertaining.' I wish the shooting of it had been that way too.

Unfortunately, I was still Hammer's production manager. So forget the fact I'd written the script, it was time for me to get back to my day job. First I had to make out a shooting schedule, along with the budget. The two are inextricably entwined. How much money do we have? Okay, that means we can afford a six-week schedule. But hang on, this picture has a lot of special effects. So I get together with Les Bowie, Hammer's special effects expert, and he tells me what he needs and how much it's going to cost. I tell him it's too much, he says tough shit, that's what it's going to take, so I have to knock a week off the schedule to come up with the money.

About then, Joe Losey came into my life again as the contracted director. Because the pressure from Hollywood hadn't got any better, he came aboard under the name of Joe Walton. But this didn't fool anyone. Especially it didn't fool Dean Jagger, the American star they sent over. Joe Walton, Joe Losey... no way was he going to work for them... him. Back in the good old US of A, the Screen Actors Guild would have possibly thrown him out and the big studios would never employ him again (at least not until around ten years later when everything died down and they realised what they'd allowed McCarthy to get away with). So Joe Losey was out. In his place we got Leslie Norman.

As I say, I was looking at the movie the other day. First time I've viewed it since I can't remember when, and, I have to admit, Leslie Norman made a pretty good job of it. If we'd been able to spend more money on the special effects, it would have been a hell of a lot better, but I think I'm being unfair to Les Bowie and judging his work by today's standards when, for a million dollars, George Lucas' people will give you 25 feet of mind-blowing monster. But, even though the special effects in X the Unknown are pretty primitive, they're still effective and, in my opinion, Les did a good job on the amount of money we gave him. So, with that minor reservation, X the Unknown turned out to be a movie that I am quite proud to have been associated with. Especially as it was my first. But oh my God, the pain everybody went through to get Leslie Norman what he wanted.

Trouble was, he didn't want to do the picture in the first place. He was a contract director at Ealing Studios, who didn't have anything for him to do at that moment. So when Tony Hinds went to Ealing looking for somebody at extremely short notice, the studios told Leslie that, like it or not, he was going to have to do it. It was a position that no director should be forced into; it happened to me many years later, so I know. The script has been finalised, the crew are all aboard, casting is completed, the sets built and the locations

*Braving the elements: Michael Ripper (pointing) and John Harvey (in greatcoat) plus other members of an embattled cast and crew at work on **X the Unknown** (1956). Joseph Losey stayed at home.*

CLASSIC SCENE

X THE UNKNOWN

*T*he scene outside the church where the villagers are all taking shelter from the approaching monster and the cutest little girl you've ever seen wanders off to look at the monster a bit closer, to be rescued, in the nick of time, by the vicar. A strange choice you may say, but you should have been in the cinema when the movie was first released. The audience were under their seats for this bit.

picked. The director, unless he's able to make his own mark quickly, is little more than a traffic cop.

Leslie made his mark right from the off by being a bully from the beginning to the end of the shoot. He took positive pleasure in treating the crew and cast badly. The whole unit had a row with him at one time or another. Anthony Newley christened him 'the Butcher of Ealing' and Michael Ripper, who made over 30 Hammer films during his career, was told by Norman that, if he had been doing the casting, he would have got Victor Maddern instead. To add to these problems it was a difficult shoot anyway. Locations were out in the mud of the Gerrards Cross sand and gravel pits, at night, in the pouring rain and freezing cold.

Viewing the picture I can't help wondering why we didn't shoot all that night location in the daytime. We already had daytime scenes out there, it was a good location, so why did the arsehole writer make it a night sequence and create all that aggravation for the poor production manager, bless him! It would have made no difference to the plot. There had to be a reason, but for the life of me, I can't remember what it was. What I can remember is night after night of absolute freezing cold misery: transport sinking into the mud; crew members getting sick; everybody complaining, even though they were earning overtime like they never had before. Miseryville.

The only good thing that happened to me on that shoot was my son was born. In those days fathers weren't required to attend the birth of their children. In fact they were positively discouraged. Monica went into the nursing home late one evening, I got a call at 5.30 am the next day, paid a flying visit, kissed the baby and then disappeared for the next three days to continue doing battle with Leslie Norman and the elements.

Still, we lived through it. The picture was completed. Shot in January and February of 1956 and released in August. It was released in the UK by Warners, sharing a bill with *Les Diaboliques*, one of my favourite films of all time. And, best of all, I was suddenly a proper, money-earning, dyed-in-the-wool screenwriter.

CHAPTER 3

The Curse of Frankenstein

THE CURSE OF FRANKENSTEIN

(filmed 19 November 1956 to 3 January 1957,
released 2 May 1957)

Now we come down to the serious stuff. Hammer's main claim to fame. The Gothics. People still consider them great horror movies. To me, they were elaborate fairy tales rather than horror stories. 'Once upon a time, in a castle at the top of a mountain, there lived a wicked, evil man/witch/monster...'

I'll admit that perhaps this theory is only valid in retrospect. Compared to the horror on screen today, what we watched way back then seems positively benign. My grandchildren watched Dracula and Frankenstein when they were seven years old and loved them. I'd scream blue bloody murder if I caught them watching one of the Freddy Krueger movies. (Though they've probably done that too.)

The first of the Gothics was to be *The Curse of Frankenstein* and yours truly was hired to write it. I learned later that the machinations leading up to this point were quite convoluted. The original instigators were a couple of American guys, Milton Subotsky and Max Rosenberg. They had a script in America and took it to Eliot Hyman, who ran a company called Seven Arts which was associated with Hammer at the time. Hyman took the script to Jimmy Carreras, who, in turn, took it to British distributor ABC who gave it the thumbs-up and we were off and running.

Unfortunately, or depending on your point of view, fortunately, Tony Hinds didn't particularly like the script so he asked me to start again from scratch and write my version based on the original book. As I said, I learned all this later. I had no idea at the time that there was a script already in existence. And to this day I've never read it. As far as I was concerned Tony came to me and asked if I'd like to write Frankenstein and I said 'Yes please.'

As for why me, Tony has been quoted as saying 'I wanted Jimmy Sangster because he was a friend and because I knew he'd do what I told him.'

Right on both counts.

As for Milton Subotsky and Max Rosenberg, I never met either of them which, all things considered, is strange. Their company, Amicus, subsequently made a lot of good horror movies, a number of them directed by Freddie Francis. The first was *Dr Terror's House of Horrors*, an extremely efficient movie with a cast to drool over: Cushing, Lee, Roy Castle, Kenny Lynch, Michael Gough, Donald Sutherland, to name but a few. Then there was *The Skull*, with Cushing and Lee, and *Torture Garden*, also directed by Freddie. Their *Scream and Scream Again* starred Vincent Price and Chris Lee and they went on to make *The House that Dripped Blood* and *I, Monster*. A pretty impressive record. Wonder why they never employed Jimmy Sangster?

As soon as the project was announced, Universal in Hollywood threatened to sue us for infringement of copyright. It didn't take a Clarence Darrow to point out that Mary Shelley, who wrote the novel, had been dead for over a hundred years and therefore it was in public domain. 'Point taken,' said Universal, 'but make sure your monster in no way resembles the old Boris Karloff version. That is our copyright.'

Peter Cushing as the Baron in **The Curse of Frankenstein** *(1957).*

The Baron (Peter Cushing) sets about his grisly task as Paul Krempe (Robert Urquhart) looks on disapprovingly. **The Curse of Frankenstein** (1957).

But that was the make-up department's problem, not mine. The only instruction Tony gave me was to keep the movie cheap. And to prove that he meant what he said, he only paid me £450 to write the script. So I read the book and put pen to paper.

The first major change I made was to make Baron Frankenstein the villain, as opposed to the monster. Let's face it, the monster couldn't help doing monstrous things. Having great body parts isn't going to be much good if his brain is full of broken glass before it's even planted in his reconstructed skull. The Baron, on the other hand, was a well-educated, brilliant, seemingly charming man. He didn't set out to create a monster, he just wanted to create life. Unfortunately everything got screwed up and that's where his true character came out. He became an evil, cold-blooded murderer. And when confronted with this fact, he was unable to understand what all the fuss was about.

The second major change I made wasn't my choice. Tony Hinds said keep it cheap, so that's what I tried to do. Every other Frankenstein movie before and since has had a bunch of irate peasants descending on the castle. Peasants cost money, especially when they're descending on the castle at night, so lose the peasants. Talk about them; hear them baying in the background; see the reflected light from their flaming torches on the trees if you like; but keep them off the screen. Also, keep the locations to an absolute minimum and, when completely unavoidable, no more than 30 minutes drive from the studio. No night exteriors, no special effects and keep the cast small.

Third, 'straightline' the story as much as possible, cut out subsidiary parts and keep one's fingers crossed that they cast the principal parts well. So I cut out a lot of the original novel's characters.

The movie opened in the prison where Frankenstein (Peter Cushing) is due to be hanged for murder. He pleads his innocence to the visiting priest and we go to flashback for the rest of the picture until, at the end, we return to the prison for the execution. The story itself is so familiar it's not even worth repeating. But I will just the same. He makes a living man from bits and pieces he begs, borrows or steals and, because the brain is damaged, the living man is a monster who eventually goes on the rampage and is finally destroyed. Apply that to every Frankenstein movie ever made, there's a whole bunch of them, and you won't be far wrong.

Between the time I delivered the first draft of the script and had finished the rewrites Tony asked for, Hammer had already drawn up a three-week shooting schedule in black and white. But Tony liked my final script enough to persuade the company to increase the schedule to four weeks and shoot in colour. He got

TERENCE FISHER

What can I tell you about Terry that hasn't been said a hundred times before? He was kind, gentle and, when necessary, as tough as old boots. His career had been a long and mostly successful one before he joined Hammer. For the Rank Organisation he co-directed one of my favourite movies, So Long at the Fair, along with, among others, The Astonished Heart. He did eleven movies for Hammer before Frankenstein. I was assistant director or production manager on nine of them. He had a lovely sense of humour. He would have been as surprised as I was/am at the celebrity that this bunch of half-a-dozen movies brought him. He missed most of the glory because you don't become a cult figure until the cult has come into existence and he died before the whole thing really started.

It's been said that his claim to fame was entirely due to the fact that Hammer owed him one final picture on a three-picture deal. But he could still have done Frankenstein and then not have been asked to do another. But he made such a fine job of it and enjoyed it so much that he was a natural for the others. He was a joy to work with and I have never heard a word said against him by anyone who knew him.

*Director Terence Fisher, pictured during location shooting for **Mask of Dust** in 1954.*

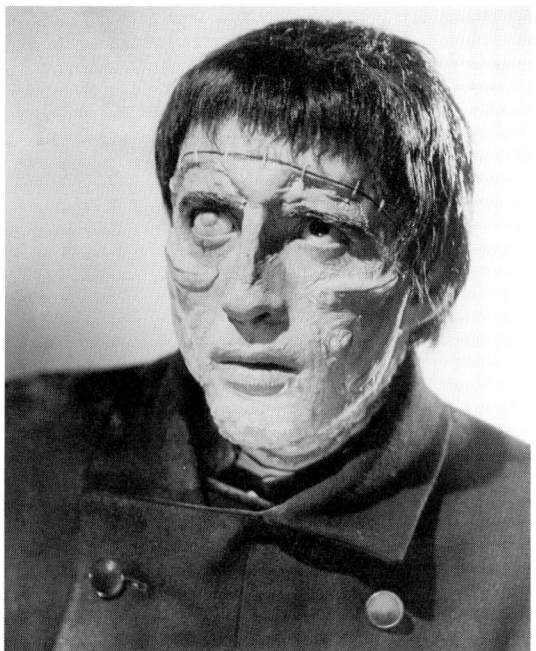

*Christopher Lee endured hours of make-up to play the Creature in **The Curse of Frankenstein** (1957).*

the okay for a go-ahead and Terry Fisher was designated as director.

Next came the casting. There was some argument from the American partners about casting a recognisable 'name' in the movie. The fee in the budget for the part of Baron Frankenstein was £1250 so that particular argument didn't go far. Just as well, because Tony Hinds excelled himself by casting the Baron and the Creature superlatively well. Peter Cushing was already

Paul Krempe
(Robert Urquhart)
rushes to save
Frankenstein (Peter
Cushing) from his
deranged Creature
(Christopher Lee) in
**The Curse of
Frankenstein**
(1957).

a star on British television. He'd won a couple of Best Television Actor awards and had done innumerable TV plays and serials, including the lead in the fine BBC production of George Orwell's *Nineteen Eighty-Four*, which was scripted, coincidentally, by Nigel Kneale who wrote *Quatermass*. For the Creature, he cast Christopher Lee, whose main claim to fame at that time was that he was a reliable actor, albeit not very well known, and he was 6'4" tall.

I watched it the other day. The first time I'd seen it since the Germans did a Jimmy Sangster retrospective a few years back and I was forced to watch it in German in four different German cities over a period of a couple of weeks. (I've also seen it in Spanish and in French and somebody sent me a tape of the Japanese version.) Anyway, watching it the other day,

as with *Dracula* and some of the others, I can only reiterate what I said earlier: the fact that they are, for want of a better word, gentle, compared with today's horror movies.

What is surprising is that they are still eminently watchable, even if watching it from this distance throws up a few shortcuts that we employed. Like, for instance, after the Creature has been shot by Paul and buried in the forest, the Baron digs him up again and brings him back to the castle. Nobody ever asked me how he managed to do that all on his own, for which I am grateful because I don't know the answer.

Another howling error is the fact that when Frankenstein first meets the character Krempe, played by Robert Urquhart, he is little more than a boy (Melvyn Hayes). By the end of the movie Frankenstein, now being played by Peter Cushing, looks older than Krempe, who doesn't seem to have aged at all beyond the fact that he's grown a beard.

This was the first time I used a 'voice over' to cover a great chunk of plot, the introduction of Paul into the young Baron's life to the point when the story actually starts.

It is quite interesting how the Baron's motives were honourable for a good chunk of the movie. He sets out to build a perfect human being. Nothing wrong in that. We're already having ethical discussions and arguments about it. First the cloned sheep! Then a monkey! What next? Victor actually says to Paul in one scene that he's doing no real wrong... just robbing a few graves. The first really evil thing he does is when he murders the professor by pushing him off the first floor gallery.

People have criticised my early scripts as being misogynistic. Watching Hazel Court battle with the part of Elizabeth, I have to admit they have some justi-

fication. It was a rotten part, not very well written. Hazel was the wife of actor Dermot Walsh and their six-year-old daughter Sally was cast in the part of the child Elizabeth. Valerie Gaunt, as the maid, came off a lot better. According to the publicity department, she was cast for her 'screaming abilities', which is a load of codswallop if ever I heard one.

One thing that stands out for me is Christopher Lee's handling of the part of the Creature, from his first faltering steps, through his escape and wandering in the woods, but especially in the scene where Victor brings Paul up to the laboratory to show him how his experiment has finally worked. This involved a fair amount of discussion between Terry Fisher and Christopher, Tony Hinds and, eventually, me. Should the Creature be savage and frightening or pathetic? Pathetic won the day, and Christopher's staggering around trying to control his limbs and obey Frankenstein's instructions was extremely well done. The frightening came later.

Still wearing his costume, Peter Cushing attends a presentation at Bray Studios during production of **The Curse of Frankenstein** *in 1956.*

But the main memory I have of this, my first Gothic horror movie, was my 'pass the marmalade' line.

INT. HALL. CASTLE FRANKENSTEIN. NIGHT.
A scene between Victor Frankenstein and the maid, Justine. She is angry that the girl, Elizabeth, has moved in and reminds Victor that he said he would marry her. Victor laughs at the idea. Justine tells him she is pregnant. And, if he doesn't marry her she's going to tell the authorities about what he's doing in the laboratory. Right then, Victor decides he's going to have to kill her.

INT. LABORATORY. NIGHT.
Later that night, Victor leaves the laboratory and Justine creeps in. She wanders around and eventually finds her way into the inner lab where the Creature is kept. She becomes aware of the Creature, who goes for her. She runs for the door, but before she can reach it, Victor slams it and locks it from the outside. Then he stands there and listens to her dreadful screams as the Creature kills her.

INT. BREAKFAST ROOM. DAY.
The following morning. Victor and Elizabeth having breakfast. All very genteel and civilised. Then the first line from Victor.

VICTOR: Pass the marmalade.

The line was put there for a good reason. I'm a great believer in giving an audience breathing space. If you scare them or show them something horrible, give them a chance to settle down again afterwards. And the best way to do this is to make them laugh. 'Pass the marmalade' brought the house down. I think Terry waited a fraction too long to have Peter deliver the line, but that's just my opinion. It still served its purpose. It was only in retrospect that I realised I used a similar 'turn of phrase' in X the Unknown.

'Pass the marmalade.' The Baron (Peter Cushing) maintains a veneer of civility with cousin Elizabeth (Hazel Court) in **The Curse of Frankenstein** (1957).

CLASSIC SCENE

THE CURSE OF FRANKENSTEIN

Needless to say, my favourite scene is the one with the 'pass the marmalade' line. My other favourite scene is the one where Christopher Lee behaves like a pet dog, obeying the commands of his master to 'come', 'sit', 'fetch'... whatever. The performance is so good.

INT. HELICOPTER. NIGHT.
The army helicopter is tracking the monster back to its lair over its predestined path. Suddenly the map reader, sitting next to the pilot, shouts in fear.

MAP READER: My God! It's changed direction.

The pilot glances at him and the map.

PILOT: The map's upside down.

It didn't get the laugh that 'pass the marmalade' did but the idea was the same. There aren't many of my subsequent scripts that don't have what Tony Hinds and I came to refer to as the 'pass the marmalade' syndrome.

The movie was completed on schedule and, I believe on budget. Everything that went on at the studio was as it should have been. Unfortunately, back in Hammer House was another story. Fifty per cent of the finance was being put up by Eliot Hyman in New York. Unfortunately when no money had arrived after 12 days of shooting, James Carreras had a panic attack. He wrote to Eliot Hyman: 'It's a wonder I'm not biting lumps out of the carpet ... no pre-production cash from you and your share 12 days after the shooting starts – what sort of a 50/50 partnership is that?' Still, the money arrived eventually and everybody ended up patting everybody else on the back.

Needless to say, the film was a huge success, eventually grossing 30 times its original cost. It seemed that the only people who didn't like it were the majority of the critics. The *Observer* ranked it 'among the half dozen most repulsive films I have encountered in the course of some 10,000 miles of film reviewing', while the *Tribune* classified it as 'the most revolting exhibition I can remember on the screen'.

Needless to say, the review I liked the best was by a man named Peter John Dyer, who, writing in *Films and Filming* said 'painstakingly detailed, intelligently written, beautifully photographed... and, above all, set in period where it belongs, this must be one of the most polished horror movies ever made... a brilliant, bleak and beastly job.'

CHAPTER 4

The Snorkel

THE SNORKEL
(filmed 9 September to 22 October 1957,
released 7 July 1958)

Some people classify *The Snorkel* as the first of what I call Hammer's 'psycho' type movies. Sometimes known as 'cinema noir'. I don't look at it this way. To me it was a straightforward murder story. We know who the killer is and the suspense lies in whether he's going to get away with it again. There's no hidden agenda as far as the audience is concerned; everybody is who they're supposed to be, unlike some of my subsequent movies like *Taste of Fear* and *Maniac*.

The picture was shot in 1957 at Bray with locations on the Italian Riviera. Even though I wasn't involved in the shooting, I was lucky enough to accompany Michael Carreras on our hunt for the right Mediterranean villa needed for the storyline. He and I drove to Paris where we stayed for a couple of days before taking another three days to drive down to the South of France. There were no motorways back then, so three days was quite a respectable time to take. We weren't able to find what we wanted on the French Riviera so, after wining and dining some more, we crossed into Italy where we continued to wine and dine along the coast until we reached San Remo, where Michael spotted the ideal villa.

'It's going to require a couple of script changes,' he said to me. 'The shot where we see Paul Decker climb out of the third floor window, we'll have to change that to the second floor window.'

'Right,' says I.

Long silence. Finally: 'Well, aren't you going to write it down?' says Michael.

After considerable patting of pockets: 'Can you lend me a pencil?' says I.

Michael went ballistic. 'What kind of a writer are you, for Christ's sake? I bring you a thousand miles. I wine and dine you like you've never been wined and dined before, and you haven't got a PENCIL???'

Or words to that effect. Maybe not too funny in retrospect, but Michael and I dined out on that story for years.

Anyway, I borrowed a pencil from somewhere and eventually they made the movie. If you didn't see it first time round, it's unlikely that you ever saw it at all. It seems to have disappeared from the face of the earth. But, as usual, you can rely on the fans. Knowing I was desperate to get hold of a version, somebody dug deep and came up with a tape.

In their magnificent Italian villa, Paul Decker (Peter van Eyck) drugs his wealthy wife, makes her bedroom airtight and then fills the room with gas while he hides safely under the floorboards breathing fresh air through a snorkel. The police put the death down as suicide. But the murdered woman's daughter, Candy (Mandy Miller), tells the police that she's sure Paul killed her mother just as she's sure that Paul was responsible for the death of her father years ago. Paul, of course, denies all this and tries to plant in everyone's mind that Candy may be crazy.

Realising he's not going to be able to do that, he decides he's got to kill her too. He prepares an alibi

Paul Decker (Peter van Eyck), the ruthless killer wearing
The Snorkel *(1958).*

for himself in France, then uses the snorkel to swim to Italy. There he makes a failed attempt to drown her before he decides to kill her the same way he did her mother. He drugs her and then prepares the room for another apparent gas suicide, taping up the doors and windows. Then he turns on the gas and, donning his snorkel, he sits and watches the unconscious Candy, waiting for her to die. Suddenly he hears people approaching so he quickly goes into his hiding place under the floorboards. The two people arriving are Jean (Betta St John), Candy's longtime companion, and Wilson (William Franklyn), an old friend of the family. They break in and rescue Candy.

The script to the end read as follows:

INT. LIVING ROOM. DAY.
The door bursts open and Jean and Wilson

come in. Wilson immediately picks up a chair and hurls it through the window, shattering the whole frame, while Jean moves quickly over to the unconscious Candy. She is about to pick her up when Wilson takes over.

WILSON: I'll take her.

They start out towards the landing.

ANGLE ON LANDING
Candy is lowered to the floor and Jean takes over nursing her head in her lap, while Wilson goes back into the living room.

ANGLE IN LIVING ROOM
Wilson runs round, switching off the gas taps.

Betta St John, who played Candy's governess Jean Edwards in **The Snorkel** *(1958).*

Then he goes out again.

ANGLE ON LANDING
Wilson rejoins Jean and Candy

WILSON: Is she all right?
JEAN: She's still breathing
WILSON: Thank God we were in time. She could only have had a little whiff.
JEAN: I should have locked her in her room. I might have guessed she would try to do something like this.
WILSON: She's a pretty bad case.
JEAN: We mustn't be cross with her when she comes to. She's sick. We'll see a doctor when we get to America.
WILSON: Poor kid. A mental home isn't much to look forward to. Look, the gas will have cleared by now. We'll get her on the settee.

He picks up Candy and, followed by Jean, they go back into the main room.

ANGLE IN LIVING ROOM
They come in and Wilson puts Candy down on the settee. Jean kneels beside Candy, just as she opens her eyes. A moment for her to orientate.

CANDY: Am I dead?
JEAN: No pet, you're all right. We got here just in time.
CANDY: He tried to kill me again. He brought me here and promised to read me a letter from Mummy. You see how he did it, don't you Jean?

ANGLE UNDER FLOORBOARDS
Paul, still in the snorkel, is listening to every word.

CANDY *(cont'd over)*: Paul tried to kill me, Mr Wilson. The same way as he did Mummy.

ANGLE IN LIVING ROOM
Three shot.

Peter van Eyck (real name Götz von Eick) in a publicity shot from **The Snorkel** *(1958).*

CANDY *(cont'd)*: He breathed air while she breathed gas, and he wasn't in France because of the snorkel.
WILSON: The snorkel?
CANDY: You believe me, don't you Jean?
JEAN: Yes, pet. I told you I did.
CANDY: So all we've got to do now is to find where he's hiding and get him to the police.
WILSON: Where he's hiding?
CANDY: Yes. He has to be hiding... in here... now. Like he did before...

She realises neither of them agrees with her.

CANDY: You don't believe me... do you?

ANGLE UNDER FLOORBOARDS.
Paul, in his snorkel, listening to every word.

CANDY *(voice over)*: You don't believe a word
I've said.

ANGLE IN LIVING ROOM
Resume three shot.

WILSON: Well, Candy, it is a bit...
far-fetched.
CANDY: But I was in here, dying.

Jean tries to take over.

JEAN: Look, pet. Wouldn't it be better to tell
the truth? You knew I'd be in to see you
early this morning and would guess you
were up at the villa. You came up here,
waited until you saw us arrive and then you
turned on the gas.

*Candy shakes her head, not believing what
she's hearing.*

JEAN *(cont'd)*: You know Candy, we might
not have got here in time after all.
CANDY: I wish you hadn't... I wish I'd died.
Then you'd have believed me. He's hiding!
He is.
WILSON: Look Candy. Suppose we could
prove to you that he isn't hiding here. Then
would you promise to forget all these ideas.
CANDY: But you can't, because he is hiding.
But, if you can prove to me that he isn't
hiding, not anywhere. Then I promise I'll
never say anything again.
JEAN: Do you mean that, Candy?
CANDY: I mean it.

*Wilson moves to the centre of the room, passing
over Paul's hiding place.*

ANGLE UNDER FLOORBOARDS
*Paul, listening to the footsteps just above his
head. He's started to sweat now.*

WILSON *(voice over)*: Well, wherever he is,
he must be in this room...

THREE SHOT IN LIVING ROOM
Wilson, looking around.

WILSON *(cont'd)*: This door was all taped up
when we broke in...
(he moves off)
... The walls seem to be pretty solid.

ANGLE UNDER FLOORBOARDS
Paul again.

THREE SHOT
*Wilson peers into the bedroom, then starts back
into the main room once more.*

WILSON: Well, he's not in there. And the
door here is taped up like that one, so that
means he's not in the bedroom.
(shrug)
There doesn't seem to be anywhere else.
(to Candy)
Unless there's somewhere you think I may
have missed.

ANGLE UNDER FLOORBOARDS
Paul, listening to every word.

CANDY *(voice over)*: Behind that cabinet
over there.

RESUME THREE SHOT
*Jean looks towards the huge, ceiling-high cabinet
against the wall.*

JEAN: That's ridiculous Candy... It must
weigh a ton.
CANDY: It'll have to be there. It's the only
place.
WILSON: Look Candy. If I move that cabinet
and find nothing. Will you be satisfied?
Will you promise not to scare us again like
this?
CANDY: I promise.

*Wilson heads towards the cabinet. Jean
follows him.*

JEAN: I'll give you a hand.

The two of them drag the cabinet out from the wall. It is very heavy but finally they accomplish it.

WILSON *(to Candy)*: Nothing there... right?
CANDY: Right.
JEAN: You'll keep your promise? Never mention it again?
CANDY: I'll keep my promise.

ANGLE UNDER FLOORBOARDS
Paul relaxes slightly.

THREE SHOT

WILSON: You know Candy, that promise could make quite a difference to your future, couldn't it, Miss Edwards? No need for any doctors.
JEAN: That's right... As long as she keeps it.
CANDY: I'll keep it.
WILSON: I'm sure you will. Let's go down to the car, shall we?

The three of them head towards the door. Just before she goes out, Candy turns back into the room.

CANDY: I'm sorry Mummy, but I did my best.

She exits with the other two.

ANGLE UNDER FLOORBOARDS
Paul breathes a vast sigh of relief. Now he starts to try to ease the trapdoor open. It doesn't budge.

ANGLE
The heavy cabinet is across the trapdoor.

BACK TO PAUL
What the hell's wrong? He takes off his snorkel and strains against the trapdoor again. Still nothing. He breaks into a sweat. After one

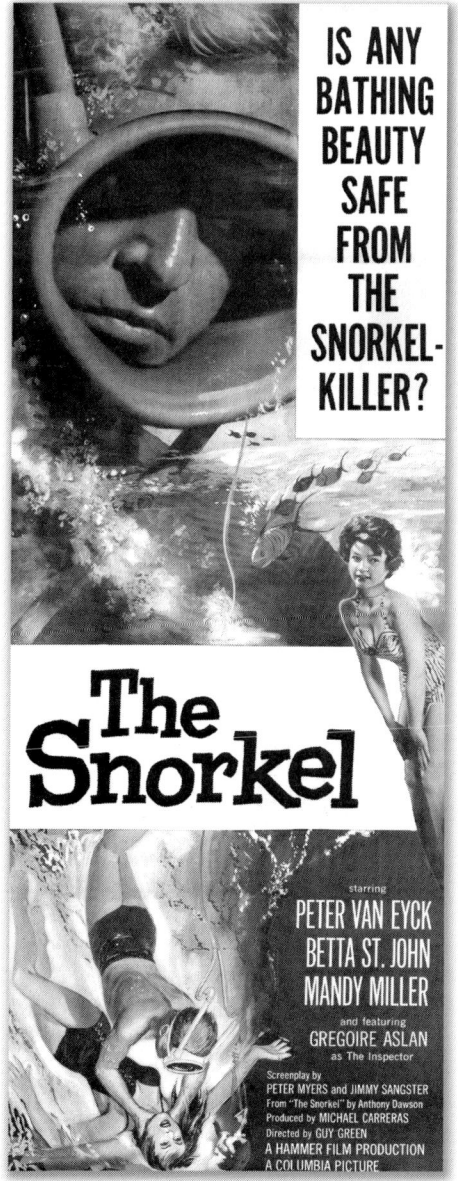

more try, he starts to knock on the floorboards above him.

EXT. VILLA. DAY.
Just about to get into the car, Candy suddenly turns.

CANDY: I must have one more look.

She starts back towards the villa.

JEAN: Candy... no... !
WILSON: Let her have her last look. Let her
  be completely satisfied.

INT. LIVING ROOM.
*Candy comes running up the stairs and into the
living room. She stops in the middle of the
room, looking around.*

ANGLE – PAUL
He's heard her footsteps.

PAUL: Candy... !

CLOSE CANDY
She reacts to the voice. She starts forward.

PAUL *(over)*: Candy... Is that you? Help me
  out Candy. Do you hear? Let me out.

*Candy looks at the cabinet and then down to
the trapdoor it rests on.*

PAUL: Candy, do you hear me? Candy, if you
  can't help me, call the others. I'd rather
  they found me than...

CLOSE PAUL
*Real terror building as he gets nothing back
from Candy.*

PAUL: Candy... Do you hear me? Call
  them...!

ANGLE CANDY
She knows now exactly what has happened.

CANDY: It's just my imagination. You're not
  really there. They proved you weren't. It's
  just my silly imagination and I mustn't
  believe it.

ANGLE PAUL
As he begins to realise what is happening.

CANDY *(voice over)*: They made me promise
  never to mention it again.
PAUL: No, Candy... please...

ANGLE CANDY
Fully aware of what has happened.

PAUL *(voice over)*: ... Let me out... Candy...
  Let me out. I'll die here...

*Candy speaks a shade louder so that Paul is
sure to hear her voice.*

CANDY: It's just my imagination. I must
  keep my promise.

*And turning, she goes out, closing the door
behind her.*

PAUL *(voice over)*: Candy... Help! Help... !

The sound of him banging on the floorboards.

EXT. VILLA. DAY.
*Candy comes running from the villa to join the
other two.*

CANDY: OK. Let's go!

*She climbs into the car. A moment later it starts
away.*

CLOSE CANDY
She looks back towards the villa.

HER EYELINE
The villa... disappearing fast.

RESUME CANDY
*She faces front again. Is it a smile of satisfaction
on her face? It's difficult to know.*

LONG SHOT
The car, heading downhill.

FADE OUT. THE END.

Except that wasn't the end of the movie. It was just the end of the script as I wrote it. Somebody, I'm not sure who... maybe it was the censor, maybe the American distributor Columbia or maybe even Jim Carreras... got cold feet about this one. Anyway, I had to write a final scene where the girl walks into the local police station to tell them that Paul is trapped, thus saving his life. It was something I really didn't want to do at the time and I still think the movie would have been better if they'd kept to my original version. At least it would have given the audience something to discuss/argue about when they left the cinema. Always a good thing.

This is exactly the same thing I had to do years later when I was making *The Nanny*, except with that one it cost a great deal of money because we'd finished shooting the movie and broken down all the sets before the decision was made. More of which later.

The Snorkel was a good story and the movie was well made. I shared the screenplay credit with Peter Myers.

'So how did you get on with Mr Myers?' somebody once asked me.

In fact I've never met the man to this day. To a lot of people, a shared screenplay credit means two guys locked up in a room for weeks on end battling out a story together. Maybe it does sometimes, but that is the exception rather than the rule. I have shared screenplay credits on at least half a dozen of my movies and never have I worked with any of my supposedly co-writers. Either he has rewritten me or, as was the case generally with Hammer, I rewrote them.

The movie was directed by Guy Green, an ex-cameraman who had won an Oscar for photographing *Great Expectations*. He went on to direct half-a-dozen big Hollywood movies. One would like to think it was because of the success of *The Snorkel*, but I'm sure it wasn't. Not that the movie wasn't commendable. The reviews were pretty good... 'A tense murder thriller' (*Daily Cinema*)... 'A first class specimen of its kind' (*New York Herald Tribune*)... But I don't think it made much money.

A word about the cast. Peter van Eyck was a pretty big name in those days, with a list of strong supporting roles under his belt. And very good he was too. The girl was played by child star Mandy Miller, who Guy Green thought was too old for the part. He

JAMES CARRERAS

Sir James Carreras MBE, or Jim to those who knew him well, was the showman who virtually created Hammer and then piloted the company through its most successful years. But, in the ten years I worked at Bray Studios, I saw him on the set only twice. He didn't know anything about the physical side of film production and he couldn't bear to see 25 people standing around, apparently doing nothing, while he was paying them a salary.

His main strengths were selling and promotion. He'd raise the money and Michael and/or Tony would go off to make the movie. He could charm the birds out of the trees, and there were quite a few birds he did charm. He was head of the Variety Club for a number of years, responsible for raising thousands of pounds for children's charities which earned him his knighthood in 1970.

He died in 1990, at age 81, supposedly with a large gin and tonic in his hand, having sold the company to Michael over 25 years earlier. Some say that he deserted a sinking ship, others that he made a first class business decision. In my opinion, it was a bit of both. Maybe we should finish with a quote from Michael, who, it must be said, never got on particularly well with his father. 'No job was too big for him. He was never daunted. There would have been no Hammer as we know it today without him.'

was probably right. But she had a good name at the time and Jim Carreras worked out that he needed all the help he could get on the posters.

The production went over budget mainly due to the foreign location work, but it still came in for under £100,000. It was premièred, for some strange reason, on the *Queen Elizabeth* on a Southampton/New York crossing.

CHAPTER 5

Dracula

DRACULA

(filmed 11 November 1957 to 3 January 1958,
released 22 May 1958)

By the autumn of 1957, Hammer were really moving. In addition to Frankenstein, they'd made Quatermass 2, The Steel Bayonet, The Abominable Snowman, The Camp on Blood Island and a comedy entitled Up the Creek, whose main claim to fame (only claim actually) was that it starred Peter Sellers. Then came what Tom Johnson in his book on Hammer describes as 'not only Hammer's greatest film, but one of the finest Gothic fantasies ever made.' Who am I to argue with him?

It very nearly didn't get made at all. An author's work doesn't reach public domain until 50 years after his death. Bram Stoker had died in 1912, meaning that it would be 1962 before his novel Dracula would become public property. In other words, Hammer had to search around to see who owned the rights. It was a long and arduous business. There had been at least half-a-dozen dramatisations based on Dracula, both on screen and stage. Hammer went to Universal, who had bought the rights in 1930 from Stoker's widow, to make sure they hadn't sold them on. Apparently they hadn't and, after long negotiations, Hammer bought the rights with one of the conditions being that Universal acquired worldwide distribution.

Needless to say, I didn't know anything about all this at the time. As far as I was concerned Tony Hinds just called me.

'Want do the script on Dracula?'

'Do I get paid?'

'A little.'

'How little?'

They told me. It was very little indeed.

'That's why we're asking you,' said Tony.

'Okay,' says I.

Hell, I'd only been writing about 18 months. What did I know about what writers were supposed to be paid?

Once again, aspects of the script were controlled by the budget restrictions that Hammer worked under. I truly believe that one of the reasons Tony Hinds employed me as much as he did at the off was because he knew I was aware of Hammer's way of working and I wasn't going to write anything into my scripts that they couldn't afford to shoot. Therefore... No nighttime voyage in a stormy sea. Better to keep the whole piece in Ruritania/Transylvania land.

I've been asked on numerous occasions whether or not I omitted the character of the fly-eating Renfield for budget reasons. The answer to this is no. The character in the book spends most of his time in a cell and would have cost very little to shoot. If I'd thought he added to the plot, I would have kept him in. But when making decisions like this, as well as the budget, one has to bear in mind the running time of the finished movie. Remember, way back then, a programme consisted of two features, along with news and trailers, so the idea was to keep 'em short. The final running time was 82 minutes. Add that to another 80-minute picture, plus 15 minutes of other stuff, and you had a programme of under three hours.

*Jonathan Harker (John van Eyssen) resists the vampire Count (Christopher Lee) in **Dracula** (1958).*

CHRISTOPHER LEE

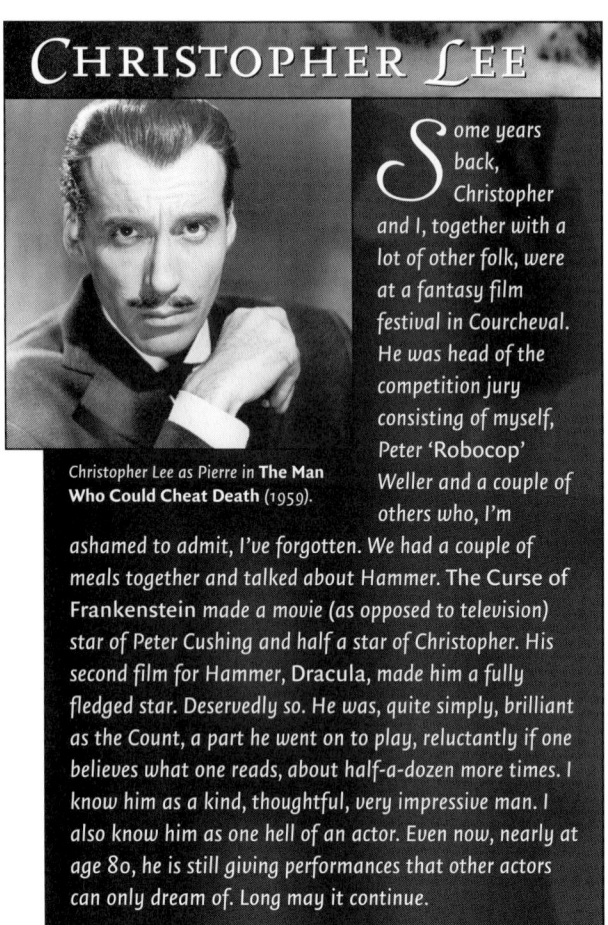

Christopher Lee as Pierre in **The Man Who Could Cheat Death** (1959).

Some years back, Christopher and I, together with a lot of other folk, were at a fantasy film festival in Courcheval. He was head of the competition jury consisting of myself, Peter 'Robocop' Weller and a couple of others who, I'm ashamed to admit, I've forgotten. We had a couple of meals together and talked about Hammer. The Curse of Frankenstein made a movie (as opposed to television) star of Peter Cushing and half a star of Christopher. His second film for Hammer, Dracula, made him a fully fledged star. Deservedly so. He was, quite simply, brilliant as the Count, a part he went on to play, reluctantly if one believes what one reads, about half-a-dozen more times. I know him as a kind, thoughtful, very impressive man. I also know him as one hell of an actor. Even now, nearly at age 80, he is still giving performances that other actors can only dream of. Long may it continue.

I sometimes wish they'd do that nowadays. The three-hour movie would invariably be better if it was cut to two. In those days, when writing a script, by the time you reached page 110 you'd better be thinking of ending it pretty soon.

Even I have to admit that Dracula turned out to be a pretty good movie. Somebody asked me how close the final picture was to the original script I turned in. I decided it might be fun to check it out. Trouble was, where did I find a copy of the script? Originally I kept all my old scripts until I was moving house one day and I said the hell with it and threw them all away. I have since learned it was a very dumb move on my part. A guy wrote to me a couple of years back and offered me, for my copy of the script, ten times what I got paid for writing it.

I finally got lucky. The script I am using here was sent to me by a fan. It is a copy of a shooting script dated October 1957 and it is obviously the one used by Christopher Lee because his name is scribbled on the title page and Dracula's dialogue (what little there is of it) is all marked.

Major deviations from my original script occur right from the off. In the original I wrote a longish scene on a coach as the occupants try to dissuade Jonathan Harker from getting off at Castle Dracula.

INT. COACH. STUDIO. DAY.
The drawn curtains sway with the movement of the coach. There are five occupants. Facing backwards are a middle-aged MAN and his WIFE, and a fat, worried-looking MERCHANT. Facing forwards, one in each corner, with a good space between them, is a PRIEST and JONATHAN HARKER.

There is a certain atmosphere on the coach, rather as though there had been long and heated arguments and now everyone is resting and restoring themselves for entering the fray once more.

The PRIEST turns towards JONATHAN as though to speak, changes his mind and resumes looking out of the window. Then the WIFE leans forward towards JONATHAN.

WIFE: Young man...

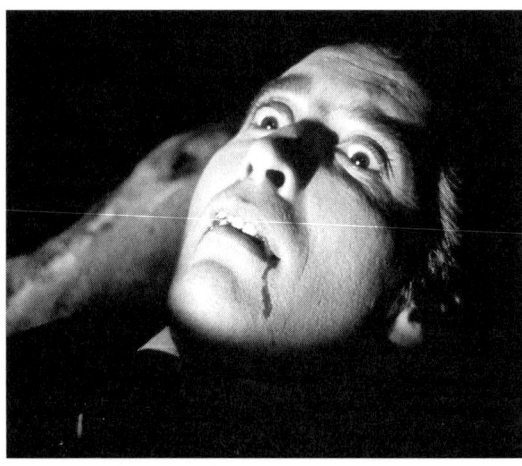

The Count (Christopher Lee) wakes from his slumbers in **Dracula** (1958).

Peter Cushing's urbane portrayal of Van Helsing in **Dracula** *(1958) represented a bold new interpretation of the character.*

Her husband reaches out his hand to stop her, but she shakes it free.

WIFE: Young man, you have... you have loved ones at home... ?

JONATHAN looks at her and nods.

WIFE: Then for her sake, if not your own. If the dictates of reason will not disuade you, listen to the dictates of your heart.

MAN: He's an obstinate young fool.

The WIFE takes no notice of her husband.
WIFE: Think of how they will suffer... then reconsider.

JONATHAN looks at her a moment, then smiles.

JONATHAN: I thank you, madam, for your

concern. But your husband is right. I'm an obstinate fool.

Then the priest has a go at him along with the merchant and the man's wife. The priest finally tells Jonathan that the place to which he is going is the gate of Hell itself where the powers of darkness and evil are paramount... and he is interrupted by the coachman asking Jonathan if this is where he still wants to get off. As we all know, he does. All this has been replaced in the film by Harker's voice over.

CLOSE SHOT – HARKER'S DIARY

HARKER *(voice over)*: The diary of Jonathan Harker. Third of May, 1885.

LONG SHOT – COACH

HARKER *(voice over)*: At last my long journey is drawing to a close. What the

*Valerie Gaunt as the mysterious vampire woman in **Dracula** (1958).
Valerie had previously played the Baron's mistress Justine in
The Curse of Frankenstein (1957).*

A coach, possibly with back projection, five actors, half a day to shoot it… lotsa money. I see from an original cast list that all these parts were cast, so it was possibly the schedule that forced them to cut it. One of the rare occasions when budgetary restrictions actually improve on the original.

A word on John van Eyssen here. He was an extremely nice man who later gave up the acting side of the business and ended up as head of Columbia Pictures in the UK. He died several years ago. Like I said, a nice man. And excellent in the part of Harker.

After the confrontational scene with Dracula, where Harker passes out, my script took a straight dissolve to his bedroom the next morning. The director or the editor decided to put in an exterior establishing shot of the house, day, as a bridge. This was a good idea.

The next change from the script was obviously made by Terry Fisher, probably on the set while he was shooting. Page 25 of my script had Harker turn from the coffin of the woman he has just staked to discover that the coffin of Dracula is empty. The script, as written, then goes to…

eventual end will be, I cannot see. But whatever may happen, I can rest secure I will have done all in my power to achieve success.

LONG SHOT – HARKER – ON FOOT

HARKER *(voice over)*: The last lap of my journey from the village of Clausenberg proved to be more difficult than I had anticipated due to the reluctance on the part of the coach driver to take me all the way. As there was no other transport available I was forced to travel the last few kilometres on foot before arriving at Castle Dracula.

Then we get the first shot of the castle from his point of view before we see him go in, with the voice over continuing.

I certainly don't object to VO's and, in this case, it works quite well. I wasn't around at the time, but I imagine this change was made for budgetary reasons.

EYELINE TO DOOR
The door of the mausoleum is just swinging shut. Even as we see it, it slams hard with a solid clunk and practically all light is cut off.
After a moment there is a shuffle of of feet, a small gasp, then there is silence again.
The silence stretches and stretches for as long as it can be held.
Then there is a scream, a wild, pain-filled scream, that pierces the silence like a knife. On the high point of the scream we

DISSOLVE

That's the script, whereas the film has Harker turn from the empty coffin of Dracula towards the doorway at the top of stairs, where Dracula makes an entrance. Fine, but it raises the question, where has he been? At least, it does with me.

The next scene, at the inn, was obviously rewritten and I think the rewrite is an improvement on my original. The same information is delivered, but it's done slightly more efficiently. This is where we first meet the celebrated Van Helsing, and it's interesting to note that in the script that was used for shooting the movie, his name is written as Van Hesling throughout. Did I make the first typographical error and everybody followed blindly on?

Scenes 48/49/50, with Dr Seward examining the sick Lucy, have been cut completely. Probably for overall length purposes. Whether or not they were ever shot, I don't know. But I doubt it, because in subsequent scenes, the doctor is just a rather ineffectual character and no longer a pompous arsehole as I wrote him.

After that I wrote a graveyard scene, the funeral of Lucy, where Van Helsing turns over Jonathan Harker's diary to Arthur. This scene has been condensed and shifted indoors.

But these are small changes and, as I said earlier, they in no way effect the construction of the piece.

Melissa Stribling at the première of **Dracula**, *held at the Gaumont Haymarket on 22 May 1958.*

There are a couple of scenes missing, like the murder of the man who drives the coach that Dracula eventually uses to return to his castle with Mina, and a scene I wrote between Van Helsing and the frontier official has been missed out and replaced with Van Helsing smashing the just-repaired frontier barrier as he drives through in pursuit of Dracula. This, I have to admit, is much better than my original.

The end then follows the script pretty closely except for the FADE OUT shot, which is in the room of Dracula's death as opposed to outside the castle. Better, I think. What is most certainly better is the embellishment to the final sequence worked out by Terry Fisher and Peter Cushing.

Script:

> INT. GOTHIC ROOM. DAWN.
> *The light through the stained glass window is just beginning to pick out the colours of the window on the dust-covered floor. In the centre of a raised dais, DRACULA is lifting a heavy stone trap in the floor.*

C.S. HESLING [SIC]
He sees what is happening. Quickly closes the door behind him and locks it with a large key. He runs towards DRACULA taking a crucifix from his pocket.

MEDIUM SHOT
DRACULA is just heaving the trap fully open when HESLING reaches him and holding the crucifix in front of him he forces a snarling DRACULA to let go of the trap which slams shut again. Then HESLING plants himself over the trap, looking at DRACULA.

C.S. HESLING
Staring steadily at DRACULA

C.S. DRACULA
He is looking at at HESLING, his blood-red eyes flooded with anger, unable to do anything for a moment. Then, even while he is standing there, a ray of sunlight creeps across his face. He claps his hand to his face and screams, then he turns.

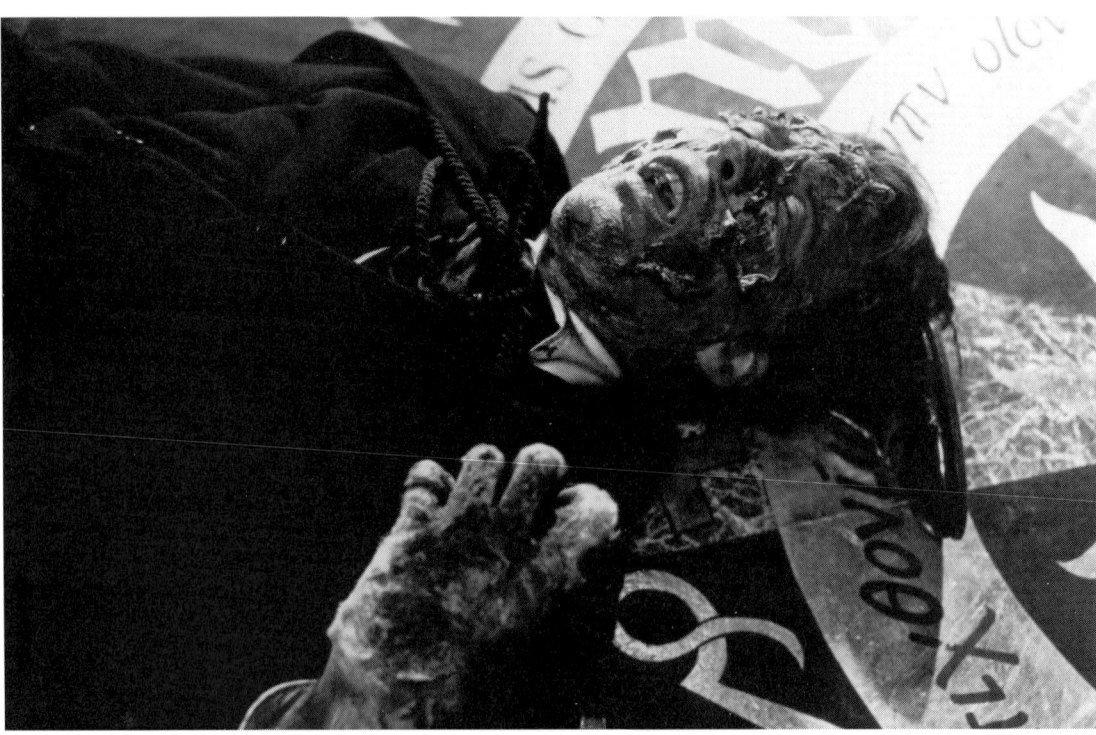

CLASSIC SCENE

DRACULA

*I*n my opinion, the best scene in the picture is the end, the destruction of Dracula. Not so much the whole scene but the bit in the middle that Terry Fisher and Peter Cushing worked out on the set, ignoring the script and doing their own thing, having Van Helsing jump onto the table and tear down the curtains to let in the sunlight. Shows I'm very amenable. My choice as best scene and I didn't even write it.

   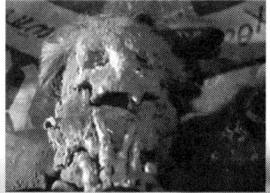

MEDIUM SHOT
HESLING uses the crucifix to force DRACULA back into the pool of light. He looks up towards the stained glass window.

C.S. WINDOW
The sun is now beaming through the whole window, the colours sparkling and then beaming in the dust-laden room.

We all know what happens next. Dracula dissolves to dust. Just as we know how the scene contrived by Terry and Peter goes, namely with Van Helsing jumping onto the huge table, running along it, leaping up and pulling down the floor-length curtains. Much better.

So! What do we have? A movie that sticks pretty close to the shooting script. But... and it's a big but... the copy of the script I worked on here was just that, a copy. In other words, all white pages. How many coloured pages did it contain when it first went on the floor? I don't know because I wasn't there, and it's far too long ago for me to remember how many rewrites I actually did myelf.

One last comment on *Dracula* concerning the reviews. I quote from a selection of reviews when the movie first came out in 1957...

'I regret to hear it is being shown in America with emphasis on its British origin, and I feel inclined to apologise to all decent Americans for sending them a work in such sickening bad taste.'

'I came away revolted and outraged.'

'There should be a new certificate to replace the X. S for sadistic and D for disgusting.'

'I can't remember being so revolted by a film.'

Then, in 1996, the movie was re-released as part of a Hammer anniversary bash at the Barbican Centre in London. Again, I quote from a couple of the reviews...

'Romantic cinema that transcends genre ... unimpeachable and unsurpassed.'

'A model of lucid economy ... a fine film.'

Which goes to show how tastes have changed over the past 40 years. Either that or the critics have grown up.

CHAPTER 6

The Revenge of Frankenstein
The Man Who Could Cheat Death

THE REVENGE OF FRANKENSTEIN
(filmed 6 January to 4 March 1958,
released 27 August 1958)

THE MAN WHO COULD CHEAT DEATH
(filmed 17 November to 30 December 1958,
released 30 November 1959)

After the huge success of the first *Frankenstein*, James Carreras had a poster designed by an extremely talented artist showing a diabolical, one-eyed monster carrying the severed head of a beautiful young maiden. The title across the top was, as I recall, *The Blood of Frankenstein*. This poster he took to America and showed around to potential backers. Legend has it that he told everybody this was Hammer's next production, shooting to start in around 12 weeks. Needless to say, the bidding started and was eventually won by Columbia. Seeing that Warners had done so well with the first *Frankenstein*, I'm not quite sure why they didn't come aboard for the second. Anyway, the deal was made and Jimmy Carreras came back to London, where he summoned me to his office and showed me the poster.

'Here it is,' he said. 'Frankenstein number two. We start shooting in 12 weeks.'

'Great,' says I, really pissed off that he hadn't asked me to do the script.

'So off you go,' he said. 'Make sure Tony gets the first draft within a fortnight.'

The two weeks didn't worry me particularly. I was always a fast writer. What had me worried was that I'd always been a fast writer. What had me worried was that I'd killed the Baron off in the first movie. I mentioned this to Carreras.

'You'll think of something,' he said, ushering me out of the office.

So, I had a couple of meetings with Tony Hinds, made a deal, and went off to write the movie.

First I had to resurrect Baron Frankenstein, played by Peter Cushing. The best way to do that, the only way that I could see, was to not have him dead in the first place. No problem. I conjured up a deformed prison guard named Karl (Oscar Quitak) and had him arrange to execute the visiting curate instead of the Baron. As a reward for this, he's to get a new body as soon as Frankenstein can get going again. Quick four or five year flashforward to Carlsbruck, where the Baron is now practising under the name of Doctor Stein. He is running a successful private practice as well as attending the poor and needy at the local hospital. He's worked out that this is an ideal place to get hold of body parts for his experiments.

Hans Kleve (Francis Matthews) recognises Frankenstein and asks to work with him. Now, together, they transplant Karl's brain into a body that Frankenstein has put together. When Karl learns that Frankenstein is going to exhibit his old body side by side with his new one at a medical convention, he destroys the body. He is apprehended in the act and bashed over the head. Still vulnerable from the operation, the damage to his brain is such that it completely unhinges him as well as allowing his body to revert to its former crippled state. Meanwhile, the patients in

*The guillotine awaits the Baron at the beginning of **The Revenge of Frankenstein** (1958).*

the poorhouse have discovered Frankenstein's true identity and they beat him to a pulp. To save his life, Hans transplants his brain into a previously prepared body. Flashforward to London, where Dr Franck has set up a successful practice.

It turned out to be a pretty good movie, even if I do say so myself. I am not and have never been a particular fan of the Gothic horror cinema, even my own. Correction: *especially* my own. I'm not saying they're badly made movies. On the contrary, some of them are very good and all of them are impeccably made. I just don't enjoy them all that much. This is the reason I changed direction a little later and started writing the 'psycho' type movies. I didn't return to Gothic until the end of my relationship with Hammer when I made *The Horror of Frankenstein* and directed the dire *Lust for a Vampire*.

But back to *The Revenge of Frankenstein*, as the *Curse* sequel became known. Like I just said, a pretty good movie. It certainly had its drawbacks; the terrible woman's part bravely played by Eunice Gayson and a definite slowdown in Act Two as if Terry Fisher (or, more likely, the script) had temporarily lost his way. But there was plenty to outweigh these weaknesses. A lot of 'pass the marmalade' material, especially the early sequence, played by Lionel Jeffries and the ever-present Michael Ripper, as a couple of drunken grave diggers, a sequence which, apparently, I didn't write. George Baxt claims to have done it and who am I to argue with him from this vast distance, even if I did know who he was.

And, to top everything, there were the other performances. First Peter Cushing, who was able to make even the most idiotic lines (and there were a lot of them) ring with absolute authority. And second, Michael Gwynn's portrayal of the 'monster', who wasn't a true monster in any way, shape or form. He brought to the role the same pity and sympathy that Christopher Lee brought in the first *Frankenstein*. The other parts, as was usual for a Hammer movie, were impeccably played. The sets were designed by the brilliant Bernard Robinson and beautifully photographed by Jack Asher. The mixture very much as before, which was what Hammer and the American money were aiming for.

It's interesting that in this movie, Frankenstein does nothing villainous. Unlike the original, where he murders the professor for his brain, the only 'spare parts' he takes in this one are from dead people. His motives, as before, are purely in the name of science. The fact that it all goes wrong is once more none of his doing.

As for the general 'horror' element of the picture, all the so-called 'monster' does is salivate a great deal and kill a silly little girl in the park. And only then after his brain has been bashed about. There were very few 'gory' scenes as such. Even so, critic C A Lejeune,

Left: Margaret (Eunice Gayson) becomes outraged at Stein's (Peter Cushing) treatment of the reborn Karl in **The Revenge of Frankenstein** (1958).

Right: Karl (Michael Gwynne), the pitiful subject of the Baron's latest experiment in **The Revenge of Frankenstein** (1958).

CLASSIC SCENE

   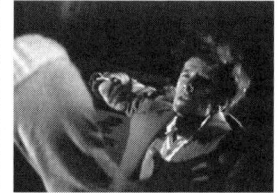

THE REVENGE OF FRANKENSTEIN

*T*he scene where the janitor, played by George Woodbridge, catches the 'monster' in Frankenstein's laboratory and attacks him. It's a good scene not because of its basic 'on-screen' content, but because the viewer knows that this quite elegant, good-looking, lucid guy (Michael Gwynn) is going to turn into a monster because of the hammering that the janitor is giving him. Audience reaction: 'Please don't hit him around the head, you'll scramble his brain.'

 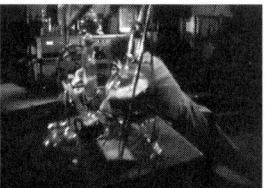  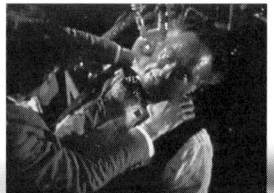

writing in the *Observer*, said, 'The whole thing is, to my taste, a vulgar, stupid, nasty and intolerably tedious business; a crude sort of entertainment for a crude sort of audience; but it leaves me with a sense of nausea rather than horror. I want to gargle it off with a strong disinfectant, to scrub my memory with carbolic soap.' How's that for a bit of overwriting?

But she wasn't alone. Another critic declared it 'the lowest level to which we were obliged to crawl'. These reviews were balanced to some extent by '...immaculately tailored, gripping and intiguing story, faultless atmosphere.' There's no accounting for taste. Still, Hammer was never in the business of aiming for critical praise. In fact, the more lurid the critics became the more people rushed off to the cinema. There was nothing better than the word 'revolting' to pull in an audience. Come to think of it, that applies today too.

During the shooting of *Revenge* Michael Carreras went off to Hollywood to shoot *Tales of Frankenstein*, which was designed as a pilot for a US television series. He hoped to come back with an order for 26 episodes, to be shot at Bray. Unfortunately the whole project ground to a shuddering halt. The pilot starred Anton Diffring as Frankenstein and when the series failed to materialise, he was put up to star in the next movie I wrote for Hammer, *The Man Who Could Cheat Death*. This was based on a play by Barré Lyndon, originally entitled *The Man in Half Moon Street*.

At least I *thought* it was the next movie I wrote, but looking at some old reviews I found one of them made reference to *The Mummy*, which I thought was shot later. Confused? Not as much as I was, until I checked further. *The Man Who Could Cheat Death* was made in November 1958 and then, for reasons nobody can recall, wasn't released for over a year, on 28 November 1959, while *The Mummy,* which was made in February 1959, three months after *The Man Who Could Cheat Death*, was released three weeks earlier, on 2 November. I guess, looking back, the powers that be decided that it wasn't all that good a movie, and having watched it a couple of times recently, I'm forced to agree with them.

The Man Who Could Cheat Death premièred at London's Plaza on 30 November 1959.

I think the best word I can come up with to describe the movie is 'leaden'. The story is straightforward enough, a 'Dorian Gray' situation. Georges Bonnet (Anton Diffring) is a fashionable sculptor, living in Paris. Previously, a long time ago, he was a scientist who, with the aid of Ludwig Weiss (Arnold Marle), came up with a formula for prolonging life indefinitely. Already 104 years old, he requires a gland transplant every ten years which is undertaken by Ludwig. Only this time, when Ludwig arrives, we see he has had a stroke and won't be able to do the operation. Ludwig is killed and Georges asks fellow surgeon Pierre Gerrard (Christopher Lee) to perform the operation. He refuses, so Georges kidnaps his girlfriend Janine (Hazel Court) in an effort to change his mind. The operation is not performed, however, and in moments Georges reverts to his 104-year-old

appearance complete with every disease he's avoided all his life. Finally he dies in a fire.

There are three reasons why I think *The Man Who Could Cheat Death* is not a very good picture. Firstly it was based on a play, and therefore turned out to be very static. In fact, the whole movie really takes place on two sets, Bonnet's house and the cellar where the climax takes place. Certainly there are a few other small sets, the inn where Bonnet picks up the hooker and a couple of small street scenes, but these were designed merely to open the piece up, which, in my opinion, they fail to do.

Second, because it was a play there was too much dialogue.

Third, and most important, I think the performances are way over the top. Michael went for Anton Diffring as Dr Bonnet. He knew his work, having just done the *Frankenstein* pilot in Hollywood, and Diffring knew the story, having starred in ITV's adaptation of *The Man in Half Moon Street* in 1957. Never a particularly 'warm' actor, Diffring had made his living mainly playing Nazis, which he did very well. I don't know exactly what he read into the part of Bonnet, but it looks like he was allowed a free rein with his performance, an unusual occurrence as far as Terry Fisher was concerned, and he chews the scenery accordingly. One wouldn't have been at all surprised if he'd shot out his arm and bellowed a 'Heil Hitler' throughout a

Ludwig Weiss (Arnold Marle) and Georges Bonnet (Anton Diffring) defy nature in **The Man Who Could Cheat Death** *(1959).*

CLASSIC SCENE

THE MAN WHO COULD CHEAT DEATH

'd like to say it's the shot where Hazel Court takes her clothes off. But that would be tacky. So I guess the scene for me is the climactic scene, the burning of Bonnet in the cellar. The fiery special effects here are first class. Whoever handled them should have been given a credit.

large part of the movie. Then there was Arnold Marle, who had been in an earlier Hammer Film *Break in the Circle*, who was so far over the top as to be practically out of sight. Again, who can you blame except Terry?

In fact, there are only two cast members who seem to keep their cool. Hazel Court looks drop-dead gorgeous and is really quite good. (Incidentally, this was the movie where she displayed her breasts, but only for foreign versions. Bare tits were still taboo on the English screen.) And Christopher Lee, playing a rather boring part, has never appeared so elegant before or since.

Another failure in the movie, in my opinion, is the special effects make-up. When Bonnet finally reverts to his 104-year-old persona, complete with every disease he'd never had, my script read...

His body seems infused with a strange inner light, allowing the bones to show clearly through the covering of flesh. His hands are skeletal things, like two great spiders. And his face is a skull, a grinning, greenly-glowing skull, from out of which stare two incredibly bright eyes.

Good, meaty stuff. But in the movie it looks as if somebody had spray-painted Bonnet's face with grey ash. Not one of Roy Ashton's better jobs. But I'm sure the blame can't be laid entirely on Roy's doorstep. Somebody must have approved of what he was doing. After all, a make-up man is a hired hand and, as such, must have all his work passed by the powers that be, namely the producer and director. At some time he must have said 'This is what's going to happen. Is it okay?' In my opinion it wasn't okay. But, in my opinion, a great deal of this movie wasn't okay, starting with the script and ending with Terry Fisher's direction.

There was a postscript to this venture. An American paperback publisher asked Hammer if they could do a book version of the movie. Hammer agreed and asked me if I'd like to write it. I'd never done a book before and I decided it might be fun. It wasn't, but the book was completed and credited to Barré Lyndon and yours truly in the US and to my nom de plume, John Sansom, in the UK. I guess you could call it my first novel. I've written nine since then and I've got to tell you, novel writing is the best... even if I didn't make any money at it.

CHAPTER 7

The Mummy

THE MUMMY
(filmed 25 February to 16 April 1959,
released 25 September 1959)

I read somewhere that Hammer's first Mummy movie dealt with, among other things, the tragedy of colonialism. I only wish I could go along with that. But I wrote a simple, straightforward horror movie, not *The Four Feathers* or *Gunga Din*, both of which did deal strongly with colonialism. Let's face it, neither Hammer nor Jimmy Sangster were in the business of moralising. We were in the business of making a living by entertaining people and we did that by attempting to frighten them. Nowadays the word 'frightening' used in this context has changed to 'revolting'. Maybe Hammer tried a bit of that in their latter days, but that was long after I'd gone.

This script of *The Mummy* wasn't based on a book, rather it was based on another movie or, as some people claim, a series of movies. Universal had made a bunch of Mummy movies in the 1940s starring Lon Chaney Jr and, as they wanted a remake from Hammer, I was told to screen them. Always one to do what I was told, I sat and watched them. At least I *think* I watched them. I know I watched at least one because I used all the same character names. But three...?

The storyline kept pretty much to other Mummy scripts. A Mummy is a Mummy is a Mummy. There's not much new ground to be broken. In this case, we opened with an ancient Egyptian sequence where Kharis (Christopher Lee), High Priest of the temple of Karnak, desecrates the tomb of his forbidden lover,

Princess Ananka, in an attempt to bring her back to life. He's sentenced to have his tongue cut out and then to be buried alive. 3000 years later, archaeologist John Banning (Peter Cushing) is recuperating from a broken leg while his father Stephen (Felix Aylmer) and his uncle Joe (Raymond Huntley) enter the tomb in spite of the warnings of Mehemet (George Pastell). Alone in the tomb, Stephen suffers a breakdown. Three years on, back in England, John is summoned to the nursing home where his father has been confined. The old man rambles on about a living Mummy.

Sure enough, Mehemet has brought the Mummy to England to extract revenge for the desecration of

Left: Kharis (Christopher Lee) exacts a terrible revenge on the Banning family (Raymond Huntley and Peter Cushing) in **The Mummy** *(1959).*
Above: Mehemet Bey (George Pastell) brings Kharis to England.

THE HAMMER REP COMPANY

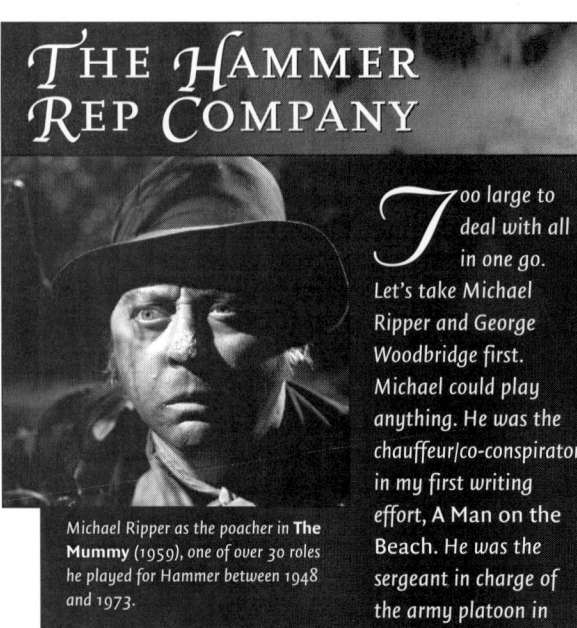

Michael Ripper as the poacher in **The Mummy** (1959), one of over 30 roles he played for Hammer between 1948 and 1973.

*T*oo large to deal with all in one go. Let's take Michael Ripper and George Woodbridge first. Michael could play anything. He was the chauffeur/co-conspirator in my first writing effort, A Man on the Beach. He was the sergeant in charge of the army platoon in X the Unknown. He was the poacher in The Mummy. He was in The Brides of Dracula, The Pirates of Blood River... and those were just the movies that I wrote. He was in many others, playing everything from a brutal Japanese prison guard in The Secret of Blood Island through innumerable grave diggers and grave robbers. He was utterly reliable on set, a director's delight in that he always added an extra dimension to the part he was playing. He was also a very nice and generous man...

George Woodbridge didn't appear in quite as many Hammer movies as Michael Ripper, but he was well up there. He was the landlord of various inns, warning people not to go up to the castle because of the nasties taking place there. He destroyed the brain of the 'monster' in The Revenge of Frankenstein, and he was the rather thick-headed country policeman in The Mummy. A very large, rotund, jovial man and one of those actors directors are so fond of in that 'he remembered his lines and didn't trip over the furniture.'

Like Michael Ripper and George Woodbridge, George Pastell was cast in parts that suited his physical appearance. He played Egyptian high priests, Indian high priests and then, for me in Maniac, he played a French police inspector. He wasn't Indian, Egyptian or French, but he always looked exactly right. He was also a very good actor and a very nice guy.

the tomb. The coffin containing the Mummy falls from its carriage and disappears in a bog. This doesn't prevent Mehemet from bringing the thing to life again and it kills Stephen Banning and Uncle Joe. John, too, is almost killed but, after a struggle, he is saved by the appearance of his wife Isobel (Yvonne Furneaux), who strongly resembles the Princess Ananka. Mehemet orders the Mummy to kill her too, but it refuses, killing Mehemet instead. Then it grabs Isobel and carries her back to the bog. As Banning and the local police gather at the edge of the bog, Isobel pleads with the Mummy to release her. This it finally does and, under a hail of bullets, it sinks back down into the bottomless bog.

The billing gives me sole screenplay credit, which is a bit cheeky if I based the story on somebody else's original. But nobody complained at the time, so I guess it was okay.

As to the movie itself, I consider it one of Hammer's better efforts. All the old stalwarts were involved both behind and in front of the camera and the Hammer repertory company was well represented by the likes of George Woodbridge and Michael Ripper. Terry Fisher did his usual immaculate job, as did Bernie Robinson. It was Bernie's wife Margaret who did the Egyptian masks. She was also the one who pointed out to me that Karnak was a place and not a god. But as the picture had already started shooting, nobody wanted to make any changes. And as producer Michael Carreras said, who's going to know the difference? He was right.

Also deserving of mention was the guy who wrote the music, Franz Reizenstein, a concert pianist who taught music at the Royal Accademy. He produced a first-class score. I'm not sure why they didn't get James Bernard for this one – he'd worked with the musical director John Hollingsworth many times by this stage – but whatever the reason, it turned out well for the picture.

Once again I wrote an insipid role for the leading lady. This time the poor dear was Yvonne Furneaux, who did her best with an almost non-existent part. As Denis Meikle wrote in his book A History of Horrors, 'a typically underwritten Sangster female.' What was it about me in those days? Still, I made up for it later, once I started in on the 'psycho' type movies. That's

CLASSIC SCENE

THE MUMMY

*T*he scene where the Mummy is busy strangling John Banning (Cushing), when he hears the voice of Isobel (Yvonne Furneaux). He looks up at her, believes that she is the High Priestess Ananka, and drops Banning and moves towards her in a gentle, reverential, loving fashion. First-class acting here. Also, of course, the first part of this scene, where the Mummy actually breaks into the house, taking the whole window and door-frame with him.

when my women characters developed balls, if you'll pardon the expression.

But the real star of *The Mummy* was Chris Lee, both for his performance and for the suffering he went through to deliver it. He reprised the details of his original monster role in *Frankenstein* – the helpless vulnerability, the incomprehension and the inability to communicate – only this time it's even more effective. Every movement he made is just right. The audience knows when he's angry and they know when he isn't. And all this he achieved shrouded in a make-up that sealed his mouth and nose shut, blocking out everything except his eyes. I didn't even have to write any lines for him. I know Chris knocks most of his 'monster' roles but, in my humble opinion, they were first-class performances. It ain't easy to convey emotion from behind a pound and a half of make-up. All you have going for you are your eyes and your body movements.

As for the 'horror' elements, in the finished product, they were pretty thin on the ground. In the original version, the cutting out of the High Priest's tongue was shown in gory detail. But even Hammer got cold feet about this one and they took the scene out before submitting the movie for censor approval.

Some people complained about inherent weaknesses in the script. The fact that the Mummy is eventually destroyed by gunfire when we already know that gunfire has no adverse effect on him; or the stupidity of the police inspector leaving the heroine alone while he goes around to the front of the house to check things up, thus leaving the way clear for the Mummy to kidnap her. But take any script and dig down deep enough and one will find things like this, either accidental or deliberate, which help the movie along. If they didn't, they wouldn't be there.

The reviews were pretty good. '...the most distinguished of English horror films... spectacular... gripping story... a sure-fire box office attraction.'

Not one of my favourite movies, but nothing to be ashamed of.

CHAPTER 8

The Brides of Dracula

THE BRIDES OF DRACULA

(filmed 26 January to 18 March 1960,
released 7 July 1960)

Believe it or not, I had never seen *The Brides of Dracula* before I ran it for the purposes of this book. And I've got to tell you, I was very disappointed.

The film began life with a script called *The Disciple of Dracula*, which I wrote in 1959. Later that year my script was rewritten by Peter Bryan, whom I had known as a camera operator during the Exclusive years. His job on the camera had been taken over by Len Harris many moons before. The third draft was written by one Edward Percy. Who? I hear you ask. Hadn't a clue then, haven't a clue now. Though the reference books tell me that he was a former Tory MP who'd written a couple of famous plays called *Ladies in Retirement* and *The Shop at Sly Corner*. To make things even more complicated, the fourth draft – the one that was finally shot at Bray in January 1960 – was polished by an uncredited Tony Hinds.

The villain in *The Disciple of Dracula* was the blood-sucking Baron Meinster, who was done away with when the hero, Latour, summoned the spirit of Count Dracula to destroy his badly behaved disciple at the end. When Peter Bryan rewrote my script he took out Count Dracula, amalgamated my two English heroines Margaret Leicester and Pauline Carruthers into the French sex kitten Marianne Danielle, and replaced Latour with Van Helsing. I've read that the Edward Percy rewrite was instigated to pacify Peter Cushing, who was being courted to reprise the role he had last played in *Dracula*. At some point between the writing of my draft and Peter Bryan's someone at Hammer House obviously decided that a starring role for Peter Cushing would be better than a cameo from Chris Lee. To this day nobody seems to know why, and Chris Lee has gone on record to say he was never asked to appear.

All I can say, having viewed the movie, is that the result of all these rewrites was unsurprisingly a bit of a hodge-podge. Not, I hasten to say, a bad picture but one that seemed to trail its creation untidily behind it. Four writers, four different approaches, four different end results, all cobbled together.

As was so often the case in those days, along with the praise, I also got most of the blame. When the completed movie was eventually submitted to the British Board of Film Censors it came back with the comment: 'The screenplay by Jimmy Sangster was obviously written by an insane, but very precocious schoolboy.' So what happened to Peter Bryan and Edward Percy all of a sudden?

One point worth mentioning is that *The Brides of Dracula* was the last of my films to be photographed by Jack Asher. Tony Hinds, always with an eye on the budget, decided that Jack was taking too long to light the scenes and could he speed things up a bit? Jack, who had been nominated for any number of awards for his work on Hammer films, quite rightly said that if the movies were to retain the excellence that he had put into the lighting, then speeding things up 'was just not humanly possible.' Tony decided to let him go.

Peter Cushing reprised the role of Van Helsing in **The Brides of Dracula** *(1960). The character did not appear in Jimmy's original draft script.*

Some critics have described this film as one of the best of the Gothics. So be it. Everybody is entitled to their opinion. And it is to those people that I feel I need to explain where my doubts lie. So here goes.

The camerawork of Jack Asher and the production design by Bernie Robinson are up to their usual high standard, but everything else, including the directing I'm afraid, are definitely not up to par. As for the script... forget it!

Maybe this would be a good place to take the movie apart, bit by bit, beginning to end. Opening commentary. 'Count Dracula, monarch of all vampires, is dead, but his disciples live on.' So even before the movie starts, we know the man in the main title, Dracula, isn't going to turn up. In spite of the legends, the fact that he was the king of the undead, he's dead. Good start!

On the other hand, there are those who say that this voice-over cleverly works in the name of Dracula thus linking this movie to the series and getting us in the mood for the vampiric goings-on that are in store. I don't agree with this. The word Dracula is in the title so everybody *knows* they're going to see a vampire movie. And now, as I just said, they also know their 'hero' ain't going to show up.

Then the coach ride, with Michael Ripper as the coachman beating the hell out of the horses in spite of the protests of his only passenger. If he's scared, why is he so unconcerned about stopping to move the obstruction which allows the stranger to climb onto the back of his coach? And who the hell is that guy anyway? A glance at the credits reveals that his name is Latour, but his diminished role as the Meinster family's dogsbody is certainly not what I wrote. He turns up a moment later to pay off Michael Ripper, presumably so that he will leave without his passenger, and then he scares the hell out of all the villagers in the inn just by showing his face. The next time we see him, he's hovering around the back of the coach of Baroness Meinster when she picks up Marianne from the inn. Yet we never see him again.

Something else that bugged me is the fact that the inn and the village are both so clean and tidy. Even the villagers themselves look and dress like a bunch of office workers. I admit I remark on that in a lot of the movies we're talking about. It wasn't until the Monty

Python movies hit the screen that villages and their occupants started to look like villages really looked in those days, knee deep in garbage and livestock.

So, on to Chateau Meinster which, in its establishing shot, looks something like a luxury hotel from a travel agents' ski brochure. But the interiors are great: typical Bernie Robinson extravagance.

Perhaps here is a good time to be bitchy and bring up some of the performances. First, Yvonne Monlaur's as Marianne. Pretty as a picture, but with very little talent. Or maybe she had talent and Terry Fisher just couldn't bring it out. Freda Jackson as Greta the housekeeper – like I said about Arnold Marle, so far over the top as to be practically out of sight – and Martita Hunt as the Baroness looking as if she's been pickled in aspic. David Peel's Baron Meinster is okay, but only just.

Anyway, on with the story. Marianne flees Chateau Meinster and we go to the big scene between the Baroness and Greta where the plot is explained. And suddenly it's the next morning and poor Marianne is lying unconscious in the middle of the forest waiting to be discovered by Van Helsing who happens to be driving by. Why is she unconscious? What happened to her? I would never have written such a non-event sequence like the one that's in the movie.

During the research for this book I looked at *The Disciple of Dracula* for the first time in well over 40 years. There are a lot of differences between this script and what eventually made it on screen, and they begin on page one:

EXT. CHURCHYARD. DAY. (LOCATION)
The year is 1895. The place, somewhere in Europe.

We are shooting through the triangle formed by a shovel stuck in a mound of earth, the ground, and the lower half of a man who is leaning on the shovel.

What we can see of the man puts him down as a gravedigger; his clothes are those worn by a labourer.

Through the triangle, about twenty-five feet away, there are three people gathered round an open grave.

They are a PRIEST and an elderly couple,

Noel Howlett, Olga Dickie and Clifford Evans in the opening sequence of **The Kiss of the Vampire**, *a scene that originated in Jimmy's* 1959 *script,* **The Disciple of Dracula**.

obviously a Mother and Father. Although we cannot hear the PRIEST other than as a mumble in the background, he is performing the closing acts of a funeral ceremony. As we see him, he is scattering earth into the grave.

Over all is the monotonous tolling of a solitary bell at fifteen second intervals. There is no music.

As the PRIEST scatters the earth into the grave and mumbles the last few words of the ceremony, the gravedigger in foreground scratches his bottom surreptitiously, and shifts his feet slightly. He is restless and impatient to get on with his job.

Now the PRIEST shuts his prayer-book, and turning to the couple he says something, and the three of them turn from the grave and start to move away, the man with his arm around the woman.

At this, the gravedigger pulls his shovel clear of the mound of earth and starts towards the

grave. We see that his shovel is the type where the blade is like an inverted 'spade' in a deck of cards, coming to a point.

As he heads towards the grave, still with his back to CAMERA, we

CUT TO:
C.S.PRIEST AND COUPLE.
Avoiding the grave in the background. We see that the woman is weeping copiously, while the man is doing his best to comfort her.

Then from o.s. there is a sudden crash, followed immediately by a long scream of agony. A female scream.

EXT. CHURCHYARD. DAY. (LOCATION)

C.S.PRIEST AND COUPLE (cont'd)
The trio stop short in shocked amazement, then they turn towards the grave.

L.B. GRAVE.
Their eyeline. It shows the gravedigger just disappearing into the bushes that border the churchyard. We notice now, if we haven't already done so, that he moves with a limp.

MEDIUM SHOT
The trio start to move towards the grave quickly. They reach the edge and look down.

INT. GRAVE. DAY.
Their eyeline.
   It shows the coffin, with the handle of the shovel sticking out of the lid. The shovel has obviously been driven hard into the coffin. So hard that the blade has disappeared and only the top eighteen inches of the handle remain in view.
   Around the hole in the lid of the coffin where the shovel protrudes there is a redness welling up from inside the coffin, spilling out across the shattered lid.

C.S. TRIO.
As though from inside the grave. They are looking down towards CAMERA.
   Now the woman claps her hand over her mouth and starts to scream.

C.S. COFFIN.
As before. And over this, with the blood continuing to seep out around the handle of the shovel, we bring in our MUSIC, and our

TITLES

This scene was entirely dropped during the rewrites, although Tony Hinds later salvaged it, with modifications, for his own screenplay for a movie called *The Kiss of the Vampire.*

   Back to *The Brides of Dracula*: Marianne Danielle meets Van Helsing when he discovers her, unconscious, in the forest following her flight from Chateau Meinster. But how does she get into such a state, and why is she unconscious? In *The Disciple of Dracula*, Maggy gets a job at the Chateau as the companion of the Baroness while her friend Pauline goes on to the finishing school at Badstein to take up her teaching position. The naïve Maggy releases the imprisoned Baron, who goes on to take a bite out of his own mother (which is a strict no-no in Vampire Land, but more of that later). Now aware of the terrible chain of events she has instigated, a guilty and terrified Maggy runs for her life. This is what happened next in my original script:

EXT. CHATEAU MEINSTER. NIGHT.
MAGGY comes running from the Chateau, heading for the road. With the Chateau looming starkly in the high background, MAGGY's figure can be seen running down the road as though the Hounds of Hell were after her.

C.S. MAGGY.
Running frantically... now she starts to slow down a little. Then she stops, listening. We hear coming towards us the sound of a horse and carriage.

MEDIUM SHOT
MAGGY moves out to the centre of the road as a one-horse carriage rounds the bend coming towards her.
   She waves her arms over her head, and the carriage comes to a stop just in front of her.
   She moves round the side so that she can talk to the driver.

MAGGY: Please... you must help me... I've
   got to...

The driver leans forward into view.

C.S. BARON.
His mouth and chin are wet with the smearings of fresh blood.
   He smiles at MAGGY and we notice for the first time the extraordinary size of his two canine teeth.

BARON: Yes, my dear...

C.S. MAGGY.
Her hands go to her mouth in horror, then she turns and runs.

MEDIUM SHOT
The BARON half gets out of his carriage to follow her.

   Frantic, she turns off the road and strikes into the woods.

   Again she runs as though the Hounds of Hell were at her heels.

   Brambles catch at her dress and cloak, snagging it; her hair starts to fall loose.

   Still she ploughs on, every now and then looking back over her shoulder.

   Then sheer exhaustion starts to slow her down, and at the same time she begins to wonder whether she is in fact being chased.

   Finally she stops, leaning up against a tree, her breath coming painfully.

   She tries to listen, and has to hold her breath to do so.

   Then after a moment, when there is no apparent sound of pursuit, she levers herself upright and starts to continue through the wood, this time walking.

EXT. COURTYARD. INN. DAY. (DAWN)
The courtyard is empty except for a coach and a groom. The groom has just harnessed two horses into the coach, now he moves off to collect the other two from the stables at the rear.

   As he does so, MAGGY appears in the gate to the courtyard. She half-walks, half-runs towards the door of the Inn.

   She is about to go in when a sound pulls her round and faces her towards the gates again.

   It is a crowd noise, the sound of an approaching group of people who are murmuring angrily amongst themselves.

   MAGGY steps out of the door again, and starts towards the gates to meet the crowd. Then as the leaders of the crowd turn into the gate, MAGGY is suddenly grabbed by someone out of frame and dragged back into the seclusion of a small porch.

David Peel as toothsome terror Baron Meinster in **The Brides of Dracula** (1960).

   She turns frightened, to find that it is LATOUR standing with her, one hand on her arm.

   Before she can say anything he puts one finger to his lips and indicates the crowd.

   In spite of herself MAGGY looks back towards the crowd, remaining silent.

   Approaching the Inn is a crowd of about twenty villagers.

   Carried shoulder-high on a board is the body of a young girl, her hair streaming down over the edge of the board. She is waxen in death, her nightdress covered with speckles of her own blood.

   As she is carried close to CAMERA, we see the source of egress of all this blood. There is the small double puncture mark high on her neck.

   She is carried by, and into, the Inn. The crowd file in behind her, muttering amongst themselves.

MAGGY AND PAULINE

Yvonne Monlaur as Parisian schoolteacher Marianne Danielle in **The Brides of Dracula** (1960). The character was an amalgam of two characters Jimmy had created for **The Disciple of Dracula** in 1959.

The heroine in The Brides of Dracula was Marianne Danielle, played by Yvonne Monlaur, but the leads in The Disciple of Dracula were Margaret Leicester ('about 22, dark and attractive in a slightly sulky fashion') and Pauline Carruthers ('about 17, fair and very pretty'). They are introduced early on in the story, when they meet vampire hunter Latour inside a coach destined for Badstein:

LATOUR: Perhaps you will allow me to introduce myself. My name is Gabriel

Jacques, Pierrepoint Latour ... at your service.

MAGGY looks pointedly out of the window. PAULINE hesitates for a moment, then she speaks.

PAULINE: My name is Pauline Carruthers; this is Margaret Leicester.
LATOUR: Enchanted. What, may I ask, are two such charming English ladies doing in this part of the world?
PAULINE: We're going to Badstein.
LATOUR: Of course, the school?
PAULINE: You know the school?
LATOUR: By reputation only, of course. It is ... what do you call it in English ... a finishing school. The last stopping place before starting out in life, and they call it a 'finishing' school.

PAULINE smiles.

LATOUR: You are both fortunate ... it is an expensive establishment I understand.
MAGGY: I'm not going.
LATOUR: I'm sorry... I understood...
PAULINE: I'm going. Maggy... Miss Leicester is keeping me company on the journey.
LATOUR: A chaperone...

He laughs.

MAGGY: Why are you amused?
LATOUR: Only the English would think of chaperoning a beautiful young lady with one equally beautiful.

C.S. MAGGY AND LATOUR.

MAGGY: Who is she?
LATOUR: One of the village girls.
MAGGY: I must tell them...

She starts out of the porch, but LATOUR grabs her arm and pulls her back in.

LATOUR: Wait. The word of the Chateau is law down here. If a stranger attempted to enlist the aid of the villagers against a member of the Meinster family ... however justifiably ... the villagers would hand that stranger back to the family. If I were a stranger in such a position, do you know what I would do? ... I would leave the village as quickly and as quietly as I could...

MAGGY: But the Baron is...

LATOUR: Please! Please don't tell me an thing, my dear. I like it here, I have no cause to leave.

EXT. COURTYARD. INN. DAY. (DAWN)
C.S. MAGGY AND LATOUR.

MAGGY: These people are human beings, they must have some respect for what is right. I'm going to tell them...

MEDIUM SHOT
She steps from the porch at the same time as TWO MEN come from the door of the Inn. They both see her simultaneously.

C.S. TWO MEN.

FIRST MAN: It's her... her from the Chateau...

He crosses himself furiously.

SECOND MAN: Let's tell the others... quick...

They duck back into the Inn.

MEDIUM SHOT
LATOUR puts a hand on MAGGY's arm.

LATOUR: Quick... into the coach...

He opens the door of the coach and a bewildered MAGGY allows herself to be pushed in.

Not wanting to arouse the suspicion of the villagers, Maggy invents a story – she had hoped to meet her fiancé in the village, but he failed to show up. She now intends to go to Badstein to be reunited with her friend Pauline at the finishing school. The Langs, the owners of the school, accompany her on the journey and offer her a job teaching English.

The Baron follows, and three days later arrives at the school pretending to be Maggy's fiancé. The Langs are delighted to meet him, but the Baron abuses their trust and as soon as he is alone with the girl he bites her on the neck. Maggy procures girls for her bloodthirsty 'fiancé' until Latour arrives at the school. Initially accused of being a peeping tom, Latour continues an investigation that confirms his worst suspicions of Baron Meinster.

In the finished film, Marianne is surprised and delighted to see the Baron when he turns up at the school. This makes absolutely no sense, until you consider that the character Marianne has a split personality (split between the two girls in my script) and in this scene in the finished film she is behaving like Pauline, not Maggy.

The biggest difference between what I wrote and what eventually appeared on screen occurs in the final act, when Latour magically summons Count Dracula to take revenge on Baron Meinster. Hardly any of this made it into the finished movie although, like my opening sequence, some of it found its way into *The Kiss of the Vampire*. My script ends when Maggy dupes her friend Pauline to come with her to the nearby windmill where her 'fiancé' is lying in his coffin. Pauline has been suspicious of her friend for some time but she goes along with the plan and is eventually confronted by Meinster, who eyes her hungrily. Latour, meanwhile, is elsewhere, summoning rein-forcements:

INT. CELL. NIGHT.

LATOUR: ... and as it is so written in the Black Book ... with these words I summon you to appear before me...

He stops reading and looks up. The cell is empty apart from himself.

LATOUR: Mistake somewhere ... start again...

He turns back a page or two, and gets ready to start again...
    Then CAMERA eases back slightly and discloses in foreground a tall, silent figure dressed in a black cloak.

DRACULA: I am here...

LATOUR looks up towards the voice, and jumps with shock.

C.S. DRACULA.
This is the Father of all evil. His face, relaxed though it is, is etched with lines of vicious, abnormal power. The eyes glean from a pallid face, the tops of his two canine teeth are just visible lying on his lower lip. There is a greenish tinge to the unhealthy whiteness of his skin.
    There is a low angle shot serving to emphasise the height of DRACULA.

C.S. LATOUR.
In spite of himself, he is in awe of what he has conjured up. Ho looks at Dracula for a long beat, then he remembers what he wants.

LATOUR: I have summoned you, Father of Evil, to hear this ... a spawn of your vile breed has violated the fundamental laws and infamous creed laid down by yourself. I have summoned you to see that he does not go unpunished for what he has done. Were I so able, I would attend to him myself as I have attended to countless others, but I an not so able. Consequently I have done what I have refrained from doing before. I have called you out of the Necropolis of the Evil One ... I have...

C.S. DRACULA.

DRACULA: I am here ... say what you have to.

MEDIUM SHOT
Across the back of DRACULA.

LATOUR: There is the one who calls himself the Baron Meinster...

INT. WINDMILL. NIGHT.
PAULINE is sitting on the box. MAGGY is standing. The BARON is walking up and down while he talks, enjoying every moment of it.

BARON: ...and it was a case of love at first sight, as you can see, my dear...

Now he turns to MAGGY.

BARON: I am sure Pauline and I know each other well enough for you to leave us now, my dear.

MAGGY reluctantly starts towards the door.

PAULINE: I'm sorry... I don't think...
BARON: Margaret has to go, don't you, Margaret?
MAGGY: Yes.

PAULINE stands up.

PAULINE: Perhaps I should...

The BARON takes her arm.

BARON: You stay with me...
PAULINE: But...
BARON: You will stay.

MAGGY hesitates a second, then she starts to back towards the door. She ignores Pauline's last call. Then just as she feels she has reached the door, she backs into someone.
    She turns to see DRACULA.
    The door is still closed. At the same time as we see him, there is a rumble of thunder.
    Now all eyes are on DRACULA as MAGGY falls back a couple of paces.

DRACULA: Baron Meinster ... you know who I am?

Greta (Freda Jackson) shows Marianne (Yvonne Monlaur) what's become of the Baroness (Martita Hunt) in **The Brides of Dracula** (1960).

BARON: You are the Father.
DRACULA: I am the Father.

There is another murmur of thunder, closer. At this same time, a gust of wind starts to creak the windmill.

DRACULA: You have broken my laws ... you have done that which you should not have done ... and you have left unfinished things that you should have completed ... you have eaten of the blood of your mother...

PAULINE gives a little scream, and moves away from the BARON, who makes no attempt to stop her. He is staring at DRACULA with the first signs of fear on his face.
And the wind continues to build up, so that eventually voices have to be raised above it.

DRACULA: ...you have allowed this girl...

He indicates MAGGY with his head, and PAULINE, who was moving towards her, stops dead.

DRACULA *(Cont'd)*: ...to remain alive even though she was in your power. You have thought more of your own personal dcsires than of spreading my cult throughout the world. You cannot remain among the Undead. I have come out from the Darkness to destroy you.

Here, the BARON starts to back away.

BARON: No... I didn't mean...
DRACULA: To destroy you...

He raises his hand and points a finger at the BARON.

DRACULA *(cont'd)*: ...die now, Baron Meinster ... leave the world of the shadows

... you are sentenced and executed ... die now.

C.S. BARON.

BARON: No...

Then he realises that he is in fact dying.
   Across the back of each hand anpears a smear of blood. He raises them and looks at them as the flow of blood increases.
   At the same time it appears on his cheeks and forehead, first a smear, then building up to a steady flow.
   The blood is coming from the pores of the skin, from the eyes, from the ears, the nostrils, the mouth.
   It flows in an ever-increasing tide, while the BARON starts to writhe in agony, a strange, half-animal sound bubbling fron his mouth.

C.S. TWO GIRLS.
Watching in incredulous horror.

C.S. DRACULA
Watching, his face inscrutably evil.
   Behind him, through an open door, we see a vivid flare of lightning, followed by giant clap of thunder. All around, the windmill is creaking in protest at the wind which is tearing at its foundations.

C.S. BARON.
He has fallen to his knees now, the blood streaming out of him in an ever-widening pool at his feet.
   Now, with a last anguished look at Dracula, he topples over sideways, twitches a couple of times and lies still while the blood that has been pouring from him abates in its flow.

C.S. TWO GIRLS.
They are still staring at what is left of the BARON. Now MAGGY suddenly puts a hand to her throat as though she has been stung.
   Finally they turn slowly to look at Dracula.

C.S. DOORWAY.
It is empty. There is another crash of thunder, a flash of lightning, and another crack as some overstrained timber in the construction of the windmill gives way.

C.S. GIRLS.
It is PAULINE who pulls herself together first.

PAULINE: Quick...

She runs for the door, then looks back as MAGGY stays where she is, looking at the BARON.
   PAULINE rushes back, grabs MAGGY's arm, and drags her to the door and out.

C.S. BARON.
Lying in a pool of his own blood, As we see him, there is another rending crash from above, and a giant timber falls across the bloodless body.

EXT. WINDMILL. NIGHT
The two girls, running from the windmill, the thunder crashing around them, the wind practically blowing them off their feet.
   Then MAGGY stops, and for a moment resists all PAULINE's efforts to drag her on.
   Both girls look towards the windmill.

MODEL SHOT. EXT. WINDMILL. NIGHT.
The whole edifice is creaking and swaying. Now there is a fizzing crack of lightning, which catches the top of the windmill and seems to carve the whole building in two, splitting it down the middle.
   There is a momentary glimpse of the interior of the windmill, all the floors standing exposed to the elements, then the entire structure collapses in a great mound of rubble.

C.S. TWO GIRLS
MAGGY is looking towards the wreckage. Now PAULINE takes her arm as though to lead her back to the school.

David Peel and Yvonne Monlaur in a melodramatic publicity pose for **The Brides of Dracula** *(1960).*

So why was this ending dropped? I have no idea. With the benefit of hindsight I can see we may have run into trouble with the censor over all that blood, and the whole sequence would have given the special effects department a bit of a headache, but I think it's a strong ending and it's a shame it was never filmed. To my mind, *The Brides of Dracula* suffered by the numerous script changes, particularly as they affected the construction of the piece. I have always believed that the construction of a screenplay is the most important thing to get right. It is the foundation on which everything is built. Mess with it and you can wind up with a house of cards. The two major rewrites on the original *Brides* did just that.

CHAPTER 9

Taste of Fear

TASTE OF FEAR
(filmed 24 October to 7 December 1960,
released 5 June 1961)

We come now to *Taste of Fear*, one of my favourite movies. Let me rephrase that, because there are a lot of movies around I like better. What I mean is that *Taste of Fear* is one of my favourite moves made by me. I ran it the other day and even now, after 40 years, it holds up well. It is exciting, suspenseful, scary, and it has more twists that most other movies of its type. If that sounds like I'm blowing my own trumpet, I am. And why not? I have little enough to say about most of the movies I wrote and/or produced and/or directed and, for me, this one stands out.

It marked a temporary shift by Hammer out of the Gothics and into what I called the 'psycho' type movies. I called them that because the Hitchcock movie *Psycho* was the main cause of my change of direction. That, and Clouzot's *Les Diaboliques*, as fine a piece of fright movie-making as I'd ever seen up to then. On second thoughts, up to the present day.

I saw both these movies within a few days of each other and, like the guy in *A Chorus Line*, I figured 'I can do that.' So I set to work and four weeks later out came the first draft of *Taste of Fear*.

The very fact that I wrote it on spec was a big turning point for me. Up to then everything I'd written had been commissioned, mostly by Hammer, even though I'd branched out and done four or five scripts for other people. Anyway, this one I took to a guy named Sydney Box, a big-time independent producer, who, at one time, had been part of the backbone of the British film industry, running Gainsborough Studios. Sydney liked the script and asked if I'd like to produce it too. Or maybe I asked him, although I don't think I was that pushy in those days. Needless to say, I jumped at the chance. This was to be a three-picture deal, with me as writer/producer and John Gilling as director.

In fact, while I was waiting for the t's to be crossed and the i's to be dotted in the contract, I wrote the second script of the deal. I'm not sure what happened to this second script. It was certainly never made. I can vaguely recall the storyline. It opened with a middle-aged couple in a minor car accident. The husband, who's driving, sees that his wife has been knocked unconscious by being thrown forward onto the windscreen. (No safety belts or air bags in those days.) He reaches forward, ostensibly to assist her, but instead he slams her head forward into the windscreen again, and then one more time just to be sure. He is about to do it one more time, when some passers-by come onto the scene and call an ambulance.

At the hospital, the wife is found to be still alive, just. A young doctor on duty tells the husband that if he operates immediately he might just be able to save her. The husband tells him to go ahead and operate, but should his wife die then he will pay the doctor a huge sum of money. The doctor is outraged and practically throws the husband out of the hospital. Then to the operating theatre, where he does his best, but the wife dies anyway. Two weeks later his bank manager

Pierre Gerrard (Christopher Lee) ministers to Penny (Susan Strasberg) in **Taste of Fear** *(1961).*

calls him to tell him there has just been an anonymous deposit of a large sum of money into his account, 'for services rendered'. The movie then deals with the doctor's efforts to trace the husband and return the money. It sounds like a reasonable enough idea. Who knows, maybe one day I'll resurrect it.

But back to *Taste of Fear*. A couple of weeks after the contracts were signed poor old Sydney had a heart attack. It didn't kill him, but it effectively put him out of business. His affairs were taken over by his brother in law, Peter Rogers, the producer of the *Carry On* films. Peter was a busy man and he really didn't need or want to take over Sydney's business. I could see that *Taste of Fear*, which at that time was entitled *Hell Hath No Fury*, wasn't going to get made.

I say *Hell Hath No Fury*, while Marcus Hearn, in his book *The Hammer Story*, says Hammer's pre-production title was *See No Evil*. And seeing as he's one of the publishers of the book you're now reading, and knowing which side my bread is buttered, I guess I'll go along with him. Not that it makes any difference because we didn't use either title. Anyway I offered to

Jimmy meets American star Susan Strasberg at London Airport in October 1960.

buy it back for the same amount that Sydney had paid me. Peter Rogers was delighted. I made one condition. He had to give me time to see if I could place it somewhere else before I forked out any cash.

I took it first to Monty Berman and Robert S Baker, a couple of nice guys for whom I'd written two or three scripts. They loved the script but they weren't about to let me produce it. So I took it to Michael Carreras, where I should have taken it in the first place. Michael, too, loved the script and he was willing to let me have a go at producing. And why not! I'd been his production manager, his assistant director, his personal assistant, usher at his wedding and his best friend. I knew the workings of the company inside out and, above all, he would be executive producer, peering over my shoulder all the time to make sure I didn't fall flat on my arse, bringing the company down with me.

It might be worth mentioning here that there are two kinds of producer in the movie business. There are the deal makers, the men who buy an option on a script then try to raise the money to make the picture. Then, when the deal has been financed and set up, they pay the rest of the money due on the script and they hire somebody else to physically produce the movie. This is a guy who knows about scheduling and budgeting and how to run a unit. Who better than an ex-production manager? Hammer did this later with Aida Young and Anthony Nelson Keys. But, bottom line, as long as Tony Hinds or Michael Carreras were serving as executive producers, it was no big deal. It meant that Hammer would ask my opinion on casting and director and script, and most of the time they'd go along with it. But if I needed something which went against the company's policy, like more money, a longer schedule, whatever... forget it!

Having just said there are two kinds of producer I feel a need to correct the statement. Nowadays it seems there are three. There are the two I've just described and then there is the multi-faceted producer, he of many names. I saw a movie recently where there were eleven credited producers. They were listed as co-producers, line producers, executive producers, assistant producers. What they all do, or did, I haven't the remotest idea. But I'll bet there was a lot of ego-aggro going on both on and off the set.

Anyway, there I was, producer. My first task involved going to the French Riviera to look for locations. No problems there. I found a wonderful villa on Cap d'Antibes. Then there was Nice Airport (a much smaller and friendlier place in those days), a small building to represent a local gendarmerie and, finally, the stretch of mountain road for the car 'accident'. Having been a production manager, I was able to fufill his functions too whilst I was there, arranging permissions to shoot, booking hotel accommodation and the like. Then I returned to London for the casting.

I'd hardly unpacked my suitcase when I was told to go to Rome to meet Susan Strasberg, the American distributor's choice for the movie. Tough life being a producer!

I duly met Susan, a charming, bright, pretty girl who had begun to make quite a career for herself, having starred in *The Diary of Anne Frank* on Broadway and, among other movies, the excellent *The Picnic* in Hollywood. I'm sure her career was helped along by her family – the redoubtable Lee Strasberg, founder of the Actor's Studio in New York, which was attended by everyone from Marlon Brando to Marilyn Monroe, and by her mother Paula, more of whom later.

I figured with antecedents like those she would turn out to be a bit of a problem on the set, keeping the crew waiting while she searched for an inner motivation before screaming her head off in terror at finding her father's dead body all over the place. In fact, she turned out to be a pussy cat from start to finish with a couple of possible exceptions I'll tell you about later. I didn't realise it at the time, but the reason I had to go to meet Susan was that she wouldn't sign the contract until she'd met the writer/producer. I was auditioning without being aware of it. Apparantly I passed the audition because she agreed my choice of director and she liked the script. We were off and running.

Seth Holt was the director she agreed to and he sided with me over the next decision that had to be made. I wanted the movie to be shot in black and white. Somehow it *suited* the subject matter better. Michael Carreras was ambivalent, but Columbia were adamant. Colour please or forget it! I think it was their attitude that dragged Michael onto our side.

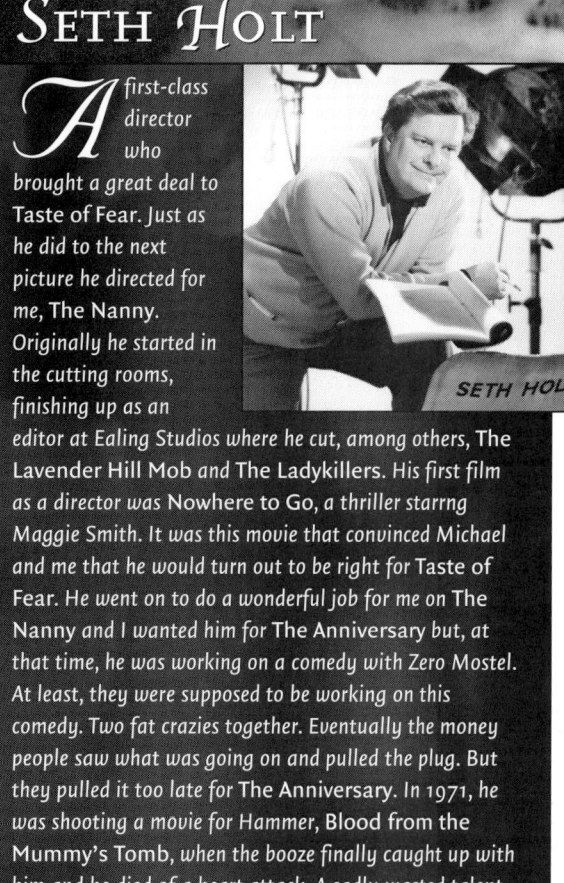

SETH HOLT

A first-class director who brought a great deal to Taste of Fear. Just as he did to the next picture he directed for me, The Nanny. Originally he started in the cutting rooms, finishing up as an editor at Ealing Studios where he cut, among others, The Lavender Hill Mob and The Ladykillers. His first film as a director was Nowhere to Go, a thriller starrng Maggie Smith. It was this movie that convinced Michael and me that he would turn out to be right for Taste of Fear. He went on to do a wonderful job for me on The Nanny and I wanted him for The Anniversary but, at that time, he was working on a comedy with Zero Mostel. At least, they were supposed to be working on this comedy. Two fat crazies together. Eventually the money people saw what was going on and pulled the plug. But they pulled it too late for The Anniversary. In 1971, he was shooting a movie for Hammer, Blood from the Mummy's Tomb, when the booze finally caught up with him and he died of a heart attack. A sadly wasted talent.

SETH HOLT

'Nobody's gonna talk to me like that!' He dug his heels in and eventually won the day. Black and white it was. And to photograph it, I went outside the normal Hammer stable and hired Douglas Slocombe, an ace cameraman who later went on to photograph the *Indiana Jones* movies. Much later.

We made the movie at ABPC's studio in Borehamwood (it would have been too difficult to build the required swimming pool at Bray) where we were quite lucky to get in. Kubrick was shooting *Lolita* on a couple of the stages, and Gary Cooper was starring in *The Naked Edge* on two of the others, his last movie before he died early the following year.

Once again Bernie Robinson came up trumps. Not this time a medieval castle or village inn, but a

CLASSIC SCENE

TASTE OF FEAR

*T*he scene where Jane Appleby (Ann Todd) is told by Spratt the solicitor (Leonard Sachs) that in fact Penny Appleby died a few weeks ago. Jane immediately realises that she's been conned, and her performance of horror, fear and surprise is beautifully done. This scene is also a big jolt for the audience who are hearing this information for the first time too.

perfect interior set to fit the Villa de la Garoupe which I'd found at Cap d'Antibes. It was a huge composite set, taking in the entrance hall, living room, the girl's bedroom, leading out onto the patio with garage, chauffeur's quarters, swimming pool and pool house, then some rocks climbing to a small promontory which was supposed to overlook the sea. If we'd done the movie at Bray it would have involved at least five separate sets.

Once Seth came aboard, we did the rest of the casting. Ann Todd, Ronald Lewis and Christopher Lee.

'Why Chris Lee?' people asked me when they heard. 'He's Dracula and the Mummy, the ultimate villain.'

For me he wasn't the ultimate villain, he was the ultimate red herring. He loved the part too. I read somewhere that he considered it the best role he ever played in a Hammer film which even I have to admit is a rather strange choice. But who am I to argue with him?

As for Ann Todd, she was one of the grand ladies of the British screen at the time, but fading fast. A former Mrs David Lean, she still lived in a magnificent house bordering Holland Park in Kensington. It was there one evening when I was having a meeting with Ann about a couple of script points she wanted to go over that she introduced me to her house guest, Ingrid Bergman. I'd like to say that was the start of something big, but it wasn't. I met Ingrid Bergman... 'How do you do?' and goodbye.

As soon as the pre-production work was completed and the set had started to go up, we took off for Nice to start shooting. The crew comprised around 55 people, so we chartered our own aeroplane, a very grand thing to do in those days, especially for Hammer who sometimes bitched over hiring a second coach to take the the crew to Black Park. In Nice, we'd booked the crew and cast into the Hôtel Negresco. I imagine we must have got some special deal because, even way back then, it was still one of the truly grand hotels of the French Riviera.

The first night we were there, I go into the main restaurant where a section had been set aside for us to find the crew halfway through their dinner. The last time I had been on a Hammer set it had been as production manager and I guess some of the crew thought I still was. Two of the shop stewards waylaid me and complained about the food. What was the matter with the food, I asked, reasonably enough. After all, we were eating in a Michelin-starred restaurant.

'It's too... too... French,' they complained.

I explained to them that I wasn't their production manager any longer and suggested they sort out their problem with him. This they did. Bill Hill, the production manager, arranged with the kitchens of the Negresco that the crew members, in future, be served strictly English food like fish and chips and sausage and mash. This they subsequently were, while anyone with any sense went out for dinner.

Our main prop, the Rolls we used on screen, was driven down to the S of F. This was the first time I used the 'buy back' system for expensive props, be they cars or mink coats or whatever. One would go to a dealer and buy the car with a proviso that at the end of shooting he would buy it back for half the price we paid at the beginning. Sounds expensive, but it invariably worked out that we paid less than if we'd merely hired the car for the shooting period.

We shot our first couple of days at Nice Airport. We'd obtained shooting permission provided we didn't interfere with any airport business. This was great for us because we were able to use all the arriving and departing passengers and airport staff in the background without having to pay for any extras. The only time we hit a snag was when they closed the terminal building one day for Winston Churchill and his retinue. I thought about asking the production manager to file a complaint, but I didn't.

Chauffeur Bob (Ronald Lewis) keeps a dark secret from Penny (Susan Strasberg) in **Taste of Fear** *(1961).*

We also shot on a cliffside road outside Villefranche and the exterior of the Villa de la Garoupe at Antibes. As far as foreign locations go, this one ran true to form. The shop stewards never stopped complaining about this, that or the other. Poor old Bill Hill spent most of the trip ensconced in a steamed-up car arguing about overtime, working conditions and the fact that the sausages at the Negresco weren't up to the level of the sausages at Elstree. We had occasional arguments with various French officials about where and when we could shoot. But the weather stayed fine, the shoot was completed on schedule and we flew back to London over a weekend so we could start in the studio first thing Monday morning.

All in all, the rest of the shoot went pretty smoothly. We had one slight problem when Susan's formidable mother Paula, mentor to Marilyn Monroe, decided to visit her daughter on the set. She was as wide as she was tall, dressed in what looked like a sack and wore dark glasses all the time. The day she came on set, Susan went to pieces. Paula sat in a chair at the edge of the set and every time the director said 'Cut' Susan would look towards her for approval. If Paula shook her head, Susan would ask the director if she could do another take. After a couple of hours of this, the director dragged me off to a corner and said if I didn't get rid of that witch he was going to quit. So I got rid of her. I can't remember what I said to her, what excuse I used, what lies I must have told, but whatever it was, it worked.

Susan Strasberg, Christopher Lee and Ann Todd in **Taste of Fear** (1961).

One evening, after shooting, Ann Todd asked to see me. She was worried about a small scene which we were due to shoot in a couple of days. It was the scene immediately after the denouement where we, the audience, suddenly get to know that Jane Appleby (Ann) and the chauffeur Bob (Ronald Lewis) are in cahoots and have just killed Penny by driving her over a cliff with the body of her dead father. On the cliffside, they embrace. Then, in the original, I cut straight to the living room of the house.

INT. LIVING ROOM. NIGHT.
Bob has just finished pouring two drinks. He hands one to Jane and they raise their glasses.

JANE: It worked... it really worked.
BOB: Did you ever think it wasn't going to?
JANE: Just a couple of times... perhaps.
BOB: Not enough to change your mind.
JANE: We couldn't change our minds... could we? Not after you drowned my husband.
BOB: We drowned him... remember.

A moment's pause as she reflects on the event. Finally she raises her glass to him.

JANE: Of course...
They drink.

That was the end of the scene. It was short and it did what it was supposed to do, telling us a chunk of the plot without too much dressing. But Ann Todd wanted the scene expanded. She wanted to show some passion. I told her I'd think about it and I went off and wrote the scene that exists in the finished movie, the same set, the same information, but delivered in a roundabout way which gave Ann a chance to use some emotion and a bit of sex. I remember this incident for two reasons. One, she actually sent me a telegram thanking me 'for the wonderful scene you wrote for me.' And, two, it did, in fact, make a better scene than my original.

The last sequence we shot was in Black Park, in Buckinghamshire. In fact a hell of a lot of Hammer exteriors were shot in Black Park. Robin Hood and his Merry Men had cavorted there; the Hound of the

CLASSIC SCENE

TASTE OF FEAR

This must be one of the scenes where Penny (Susan Strasberg) stumbles across the wide-eyed dead body of her father (Fred Johnson). It happens three times. My favourite is the one where she finds him sitting in a chair in her own bedroom.

Baskervilles had prowled the park and innumerable maidens had fled the clutches of Dracula, Frankenstein et al through its trees and undergrowth. For our sequence, which was the opening of the movie, we featured the lake in the foreground, while Les Bowie drew us a magnificent matte of Alpine peaks in the background. We shot the sequence in German because what was happening on screen was self-explanatory.

Much later, when I was in Madrid shooting a cowboy movie with Michael, I went to the première of *Taste of Fear* which had, of course, been dubbed into Spanish for that market. But the distributors had kept the German language in the opening sequence as shot. As soon as the characters started talking in German, half the audience started to walk out to ask for their money back. The management had to beg them to wait just four or five minutes until the characters started speaking Spanish.

The finished product turned out very well. The reviews were mixed, but then reviews usually are. Some critics hated it, others loved it. Par for the course. Columbia decided to retitle it *Scream of Fear* and publicise it with a poster of Susan Strasberg screaming her head off inside a series of concentric circles. It was a good poster, voted the best of the year by the MPAA International Film Relations Committee.

Then, gilt on the gingerbread, Jim Carreras asked me if I'd like to take the first print to New York to hand it over to Columbia. Purely a publicity stunt because they'd had their hands on the film for weeks already. But great! I was going to get to go to America for the first time. Then I got a call from Michael Carreras, he was going to come with me. Even better, I thought. Party time! I found out a lot later that Jim Carreras has changed his mind about sending me and told Michael to go in my place. Michael told his father that very likely Jimmy Sangster would never talk to him again and probably quit Hammer forever. I'd probably not have done either of those things but we'll never know because Jim Carreras relented and I got to see the promised land for the first time.

One last reference to this movie. Recently, Hammer has been sold for what seems like the third or fourth time. Each time the new owner announces that one of the first movies they intend to remake is *Taste of Fear*. See you in court, guys!

CHAPTER 10

Maniac

MANIAC
(filmed 27 May to 14 July 1962,
released 20 May 1963)

The next movie I wrote/produced for Hammer was *Maniac*. Sometime between *Taste of Fear* and *Maniac* they'd shot a movie on which I had the story credit, *The Pirates of Blood River*, and Michael and I had gone to Spain for six months to make the first ever Western over there, *The Savage Guns*. A lot of people give Sergio Leone credit for being the first guy to use the Spanish countryside around Almería. Take my word for it, it was us. Unfortunately the picture wasn't up to much. But this is a book about Hammer, and *The Savage Guns* was one of the very few pictures Michael made away from the old firm. I just thought I'd mention it in passing.

So... *Maniac*. Directed by Michael Carreras, written and produced by yours truly. Unlike some of Hammer's movies there is no executive producer named in the credits. With Michael as director, who needed it? But he was very good. He treated me like a proper grown-up producer, informing me up front that if I ever told him he couldn't do something, he'd say okay, you're the boss. Needless to say, knowing which side my bread was buttered, I never told him not to do anything he wanted to do. Fortunately, there was no need. In any event, I'd just been through the whole scenario on *The Savage Guns*. There, too, I was the producer and Michael the director. That time he had the added edge of owning the company that made the picture.

Basically, *Maniac* could have been located anywhere. But while I had been shooting *Taste of Fear*

in and around Nice, I'd taken a trip to the region in France known as the Camargue. While not actually falling in love with the place, I have to admit it bowled me over with its dramatic potential. To describe it I just have to repeat here the opening lines of the final shooting script.

The entire action of the picture takes place in Provence, that area of France that is bordered on the South by the Mediterranean and takes in the provinces of Vauclare, Gard and Bouche de Rhone. There is a great wine-growing area in the north, mostly flat but with occasional outcrops of rocks scarring the countryside and rising to three thousand feet or more. And in the south is the Camargue, a vast plain that stretches down to the sea from Arles which marks its northern boundary. Nowhere in the Camargue is there an elevation higher than six feet. Here, rice is grown, wild horses roam, and bulls are bred for fighting.

The inhabitants are a hard, weather-beaten lot, with little to differentiate between the Camargue cowboy and his American counter-part. They dress the same and ride with the same type of high-backed saddle. Their working lives are spent on horseback.

The time of the story is the present, with the exception of the pre-title and first sequences, which take place aproximately four years before the main action of the story.

The action of the picture takes place over a

Jimmy and French starlet Lilianne Brousse in a 1962 publicity shot from **Maniac**.

period of about six weeks, during which time it is very hot.

The story was pretty hot too, although not enough of that came through in the finished product, mainly due to the censor. It opened with the 15-year-old Annette Beynat (Liliane Brousse) being raped. The rapist is caught by Annette's father, Georges, who murders him with an acetelyne torch and is sent to a lunatic asylum.

Four years later an American painter, Geoff (Kerwin Mathews) arrives at the bar/pension where he falls in love with Georges' wife, Eve (Nadia Gray). Georges promises Eve a divorce if she and Geoff will help him escape from the asylum. He is to be helped by a male nurse on the inside and they are to pick him up when he comes over the wall. They take him to Marseilles where he is going to go abroad and send for Annette later. Then, the following day, Geoff finds a body stuffed in the boot of his car. Obviously this is the male nurse who helped Georges make his escape. He and Eve dump it in the canal.

A series of plot twists and fright scenes ensue and finally it's revealed that Eve and the male nurse (Donald Houston), lovers for two years, have planned the whole thing as a way to dispose of Eve's husband in such a way as Geoff will get the blame. His was the body in the car boot. There is a climactic chase in the caves at Les Baux de Provence, where Annette nearly gets killed and where the Donald Houston character gets his just desserts. It was an okay story, but it

Inspector Etienne (George Pastell) offers Eve Beynat (Nadia Gray) consolation as 'Georges' Beynat (Donald Houston) is brought to book in **Maniac** *(1963).*

needed all the help we could give it to turn it into a good movie.

Once we had decided on the Camargue as the overall background, Michael and I had to choose locations. The Bac du Sauvage, a local ferry across a small tributary of the Rhone, was chosen as the home and café/bar run by our protagonists. Then there was a magnificent location on the heights of Les Baux de Provence with a view to the sea 15 miles away. We shot the beach stuff at Stes Maries de la Mer, the principal town on that section of the coast. The only town in those days. I understand that since we were there the beach has been devoured by property development for 20 miles in each direction. Then we shot in Arles market and the Roman arena, where Michael and I went to a bullfight one day and sat next to Picasso. And before anybody starts to object to our patronising such a cruel sport, they don't kill the bulls in France. (Much to Picasso's disappointment.) And finally, for the finale, we went to the magnificent cathedral-like caves hacked out of the rocks just outside Les Baux de Provence.

Jumping ahead a little I have to say that, all in all, Michael didn't take as much advantage of the locations as he could have. The sheer, stark emptiness of the area, which made me choose it in the first place, didn't come across. But I guess nobody went to the movie to watch the scenery, so I'm being picky.

The story, I have to admit, was, to say the least, 'derivative', as were most of my 'psycho' type movies. They were derivative of each other and they all went back to my original inspiration *Les Diaboliques*. I'm not the only one to follow that path. I guess I just did it more than most. Hammer historian Tom Johnson says in his book that 'Jimmy Sangster's script is a miracle of false turns, and this is one trick picture that no one figured out halfway through.' That was the object of the exercise, and most times I managed to pull it off.

The plot of *Maniac* differs from *Taste of Fear* inasmuch as the victim is a man (Kerwin Mathews) rather than a woman (Susan Strasberg). The motive is more or less the same – sexual attraction of the perpetrators – and the means to this end are contrived and hopefully scary.

I guess it's an old-fashioned concept nowadays, but to me scary means what I call the 'something nasty in the woodshed' syndrome. The heroine or hero will eventually stumble across it and cope with it, but she/he will have the shit scared out of them en route, and hopefully, so will the audience. Place a raving maniac with a knife somewhere down a long, dark passage and have the heroine slowly make her way down that passage and, if you've got the build-up right, the audience will be in the palm of your hand. You can take five minutes for her to walk down to the end. Finally she breathes a sigh of relief, along with the audience, and only then does the maniac jump out at her, frightening her as much as the audience.

Then, in my movies, we usually cut away to something else. Nowadays, we see the knife go in, we see it twist, come out, go in again, while blood splatters across the screen. We see mutilations, decapitations. Think back over the half-dozen Hammer films I wrote... there were none of those. At least, there were none of those on screen. Apart from anything else, the censor wouldn't have allowed it.

Back to *Maniac*. Michael had high hopes for the picture. In a press release he stated 'It's a thriller of thrillers, so ingeniously constructed, so packed with surprises, that we defy anyone to predict correctly what's coming next or to anticipate the startling and unexpected climax.' I think those remarks must have been made by the guy in charge of the publicity. Michael didn't talk like that. Or if he had said something of that nature it must have been before we started shooting because the finished product didn't really live up to expectations. Okay, so it had a couple of surprises, but that's about all.

Not that the movie was bad. It wasn't. The performances were all first-class. Kerwin Mathews, fresh from his starring role in *The Pirates of Blood River*, was good as the slightly flawed hero, and the two women in his life, Nadia Gray and newcomer Liliane Brousse, were very adequate. Donald Houston as the villain was excellent and old Hammer stalwart George Pastell gave his customary 'foreign' performance, this time as a French police inspector.

But for a film with such a potentially vast, visually exciting background, the whole thing turned out, for me, to be slightly claustrophobic. I have to admit that this is my opinion as of today. Thirty-eight years ago when it was made, I'm sure I thought otherwise.

Director Michael Carreras and star Nadia Gray laughing through a problematic sequence in **Maniac** *(1963).*

The final film stays pretty close to my original screenplay, which isn't all that surprising seeing I was on the set all the time. When Michael felt he wanted to make a change he would come to me and ask if he could talk to the writer. I'd quickly change my hat and we'd go through the changes he wanted. Then I'd tell him I'd check them out with the producer and let him know. Switch hats once more and give him the go-ahead.

There are three major changes in the shooting script, made, as far as I recall, for the sake of the budget and schedule. In the movie there is a horse riding sequence on the beach with Geoff and Eve. In the original script it was supposed to be at night and it also involved Eve riding into the sea before slipping off her horse and taking a swim. Needless to say, she came out soaking wet and sexy. Night shooting would have been too expensive. Okay, so why not shoot day-for-night as is the custom for such sequences? From this distance I can only assume it was because the cameraman, Wilkie Cooper, decided it wouldn't be a good idea. Maybe the sun wasn't shining, a prime necessity of day-for-night photography. Whatever, the scene was shot as a day sequence. As for the cutting of Eve going into the water, maybe Nadia Gray didn't want to get wet.

This day-for-night business caused a problem later. The sequence where the two women go to the arena at Arles is supposed to be night. As such, it is very badly photographed. This time, plotting forbade us to change the whole thing to a day sequence, so it's there in the movie and to me it stands out like a sore thumb.

The second major change was after Geoff discovers the body in the trunk of the car. He and Eve drive to a lonely bridge in the Camargue with the intention of dumping the body into the river. They are interrupted by two Camargue cowboys who appear on the horizon, looking very dramatic. They drive off and the cowboys leave. No suspense, I'm afraid. The original script was, in my opinion, far better.

The car is parked on the bridge and Geoff has just shown Eve the body. They are about to drag it out when Geoff looks up...

EXT. PLAINE DE LA CRAU. DAY.
A quarter mile away, rapidly coming nearer, are two motorcycle POLICE, one the customary 25 yards in front of the other.

TWO SHOT
Geoff moves quickly back to Eve.

GEOFF: Get into the car... slowly now...

He moves with her and opens the passenger door. Eve gets in, tightly screwing herself up against making a false move. Geoff shuts the door, then starts round to the back of the car. In the background the leading policeman is about 20 yards from the car and slowing down.

Kerwin Mathews and Lilianne Brousse dance the Twist in **Maniac**. This was the height of sophistication in 1962.

C.S. GEOFF
As he moves round the back of the car, he glances down.

INSERT
From the corner of the boot sticks six inches of white jacket, jammed in the lid.

C.S. GEOFF
He looks up quickly.

MEDIUM SHOT POLICE
The first policeman has stopped his bike and is getting off, while the second is cruising up behind.

C.S. GEOFF
He bends down and quickly unfastens the boot. Without opening it fully, he jams the white coat back in and slams the boot shut again. Then he straightens up

MEDIUM SHOT
As he does so the speedcop comes around the front of the car to meet him.

SPEEDCOP: Good morning. Any trouble?
GEOFF: No trouble officer...
SPEEDCOP: It's a strange place to stop, M'sieur.
GEOFF: I wanted to see the view. I'm a painter.

The speedcop looks towards Geoff, then nods.

SPEEDCOP: It's your car, M'sieur?

Eve leans across.

EVE: It's mine. Do you want to see the papers?

She starts to open her handbag, but the speedcop shakes his head.

SPEEDCOP: No, it's not necessary.

He steps back and salutes. Geoff opens the car door and gets in and the speedcop closes the door for him.

TWO SHOT IN CAR
Geoff looks towards Eve, who nods. He starts the engine.

MEDIUM SHOT
The speedcop stands back as the car pulls away, watching after it.

So much better than a couple of disinterested cowboys. As to why we made the change, we decided that two policeman with bikes, one of them needing to be an English-speaking actor, plus the time necessary to shoot the dialogue scene... too expensive. It was a mistake, but in those days we did that a lot.

The third big change worked out for the better, which, let's face it, script changes are supposed to do. In the movie, after Annette says she is going to the police, Eve delivers her to her lover (Donald Houston) in the caves of Les Baux. There is a chase and eventually the Houston character falls to his death. Not particularly dramatic, but better than what I had written in the original whereby I conjured up an insurance policy that Eve had taken out on her husband which makes Annette suspicious and also involved another character in the shape of an insurance man. Also, in this version the Houston character doesn't fall to his death but is arrested by the police who arrive in the nick of time. Come to think of it, I think both the endings are pretty mundane, as was the movie.

But was it mundane when it was originally made or is my judgment out of kilter? Can you fairly and accurately judge a 35-year-old movie by today's standards? Take for example the scene where Geoff and Eve dance the Twist. That was sexy as hell when we shot it. Now it looks just plain stupid.

The critics didn't like the movie much. 'A plot of extraordinary cunning, not particularly well performed.' Or, as *Time* magazine said, 'Takes quite a while to figure out but by then you don't really care any more.'

One final anecdote. The day we were shooting in the arena at Arles, Nadia Gray asked if she could bring

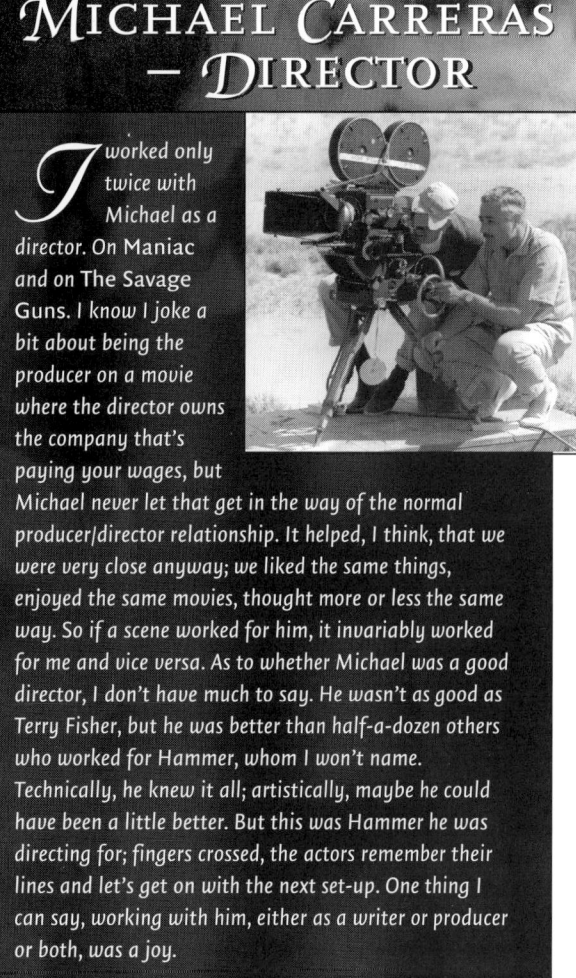

MICHAEL CARRERAS – DIRECTOR

I worked only twice with Michael as a director. On Maniac and on The Savage Guns. I know I joke a bit about being the producer on a movie where the director owns the company that's paying your wages, but Michael never let that get in the way of the normal producer/director relationship. It helped, I think, that we were very close anyway; we liked the same things, enjoyed the same movies, thought more or less the same way. So if a scene worked for him, it invariably worked for me and vice versa. As to whether Michael was a good director, I don't have much to say. He wasn't as good as Terry Fisher, but he was better than half-a-dozen others who worked for Hammer, whom I won't name. Technically, he knew it all; artistically, maybe he could have been a little better. But this was Hammer he was directing for; fingers crossed, the actors remember their lines and let's get on with the next set-up. One thing I can say, working with him, either as a writer or producer or both, was a joy.

a visitor on the set because he was quite interested in movie making. I hate visitors on sets, even though I put up with them. I told her she could bring her visitor as long as he kept himself to himself and didn't bother us asking dumb questions about how to make movies because movie making is a very demanding occupation and us producers and directors don't want to be bothered by somebody who doesn't know his arse from a hole in the ground.

She duly brought her visitor onto the set. It turned out to be Orson Welles. He was absolutely charming and didn't once tell us what we were doing wrong.

CHAPTER 11

Paranoiac

Nightmare

Hysteria

PARANOIAC
(filmed 23 July to 31 August 1962,
released 5 January 1964)

NIGHTMARE
(filmed 17 December 1962 to 31 January 1963,
released 1 June 1964)

HYSTERIA
(filmed 10 February to 25 March 1964,
released 27 June 1965)

*P*aranoiac sticks out in the memory as the first movie that Freddie Francis directed for Hammer. He'd already won an Oscar for photographing *Sons and Lovers* and before that Hammer had managed to get him to photograph *Never Take Sweets from a Stranger*. He had also directed a couple of pictures for Subotsky and Rosenberg plus a sequence for *The Day of the Triffids*.

A note in passing. It was the original, unmade version of *The Day of the Triffids* that I was writing for Cubby Broccoli and Irving Allen while I was still working as a production manager for Hammer in the late 1950s. This was when Michael Carreras caught me writing on Hammer's time (their typewriter too) when I should have been production managing. He told me to make up my mind. Did I want to be a production manager or a writer because I couldn't do both. I'd just taken out a mortgage on a new house and my baby son had just been born. I was in no condition to give up my weekly production manager's pay packet of £35 to become a freelance writer, and I told him so.

That's when he made me the offer that I couldn't refuse. He'd guarantee to buy from me one script a year for the next three years at £750 a time. Believe it or not, I could afford a mortgage, baby and food for that much money. So I thanked him very much, packed up my desk and went home to become a full-time writer. All of which has absolutely nothing to do with what this chapter is supposed to be about. A subject we will now return to.

Freddie was the perfect choice for directing *Paranoiac*. Camerawise he was a master at creating suspense. He could light a set so you would be scared as soon as it appeared on the screen. His photography on one of the truly great horror films, Jack Clayton's *The Innocents*, was the best I've ever seen. Bearing all

Left: Janet (Jennie Linden) prays for a release from her recurring **Nightmare** (1964).
Above: Simon Ashby (Oliver Reed) hoodwinks family solicitor Kossett (Maurice Denham) in **Paranoiac**, released in 1964.

this in mind, he was a natural to move on to directing in the same genre, which *Paranoiac* was.

The screenplay was based on the novel *Brat Farrar* by Josephine Tey. Originally Hammer had bought the rights nine years before and a couple of writers had a go at it. It was on Hammer's schedule to shoot in 1955 and then again in 1959, being cancelled both times. Eventually they thought maybe they could get it going as a psycho-type horror film, something that it definitely wasn't in its previous forms, and they gave it to me to script. Third time lucky, I guess. This time they made it.

I tried to keep as much of the original Josephine Tey material in the screenplay as possible but, as usual, budgetary restrictions forced us to drop the showjumping sequences which were a major part of the novel. So basically we ended up with the main framework, which was really excellent, embellished with whatever 'nasties' I could come up with. Reviewing the movie recently I was surprised to see that I have the sole writing credit. 'Screenplay by Jimmy Sangster.' Josephine Tey doesn't get a look in.

Briefly, my storyline starts with a memorial service for John and Mary Ashby who died 11 years before. Attending the service are the surviving Ashby children, now grown up: Eleanor (Janette Scott) and Simon (Oliver Reed). At the service the priest lets us know there was another brother, Tony, who killed himself years ago. Eleanor glimpses a shadowy figure in the church whom she swears is her long-dead brother Tony. This gives Simon and their Aunt Harriet (Sheila Burrell) further proof that Eleanor is on the edge of insanity. Later Tony turns up, proving her right. Then, halfway through the story, we the audience learn that Tony is an imposter, set up by the son of the family solicitor so that he can rifle the estate which is due to mature in three weeks. Eventually Tony admits to Eleanor that he is an imposter and, in due course, Simon is unmasked as a maniac who murdered the real Tony and bricked the body up in the family chapel.

Years later the BBC did a four-part series of the original *Brat Farrar*, taken straight from the novel. Any resemblance between that and the above was purely

Simon Ashby (Oliver Reed) loses his grip on his sanity in **Paranoiac**.

CLASSIC SCENE

PARANOIAC

*T*he scene where the car, driven by Eleanor (Janette Scott), practically slides over the edge of the cliff because the engine has been messed with by Simon (Oliver Reed), who is determined to get rid of the imposter posing as his brother, even if it means his sister dies too. Given the usual budgetary and scheduling restrictions that must have been placed on Freddie Francis, he managed to construct this scene extremely well, giving it genuine suspense.

coincidental. Hammer wanted a psycho-type horror film and that's what they got.

The cast were excellent, notably Janette Scott and, straight from *Maniac*, Liliane Brousse. But it was the young Oliver Reed who stole the picture. He gave a really great, over-the-top performance as the crazy young Simon Ashby. The critics went crazy for him. *Variety* said 'Reed plays with demonic skill.'

As for the movie as a whole, they weren't quite so kind. 'Hammer has come tantalisingly close to a bullseye' (*New York Times*). 'Idiotically entertaining, provided, of course, that you can find entertainment in blood, gore and lunacy' (*New York Herald Tribune*). 'Bizarre, far-fetched and tasteless' (*Monthly Film Bulletin*). All of which, on second reading, I imagine did the picture no harm whatsoever.

Not being the producer, I wasn't involved in the day-to-day shooting of the movie, but I knew most of the people who were. Apart from Freddie, who became a great mate later, the usual Hammer band were there. Arthur Grant on camera, Bernie Robinson

making sure the sets looked liked they belonged in a movie with 20 times the budget, Roy Ashton on make-up, who constructed the most perfect rotting corpse. (It scared one of the studio cleaners half to death when she spotted it one morning sitting in Roy's make-up chair.) Oliver Reed became a friend later,

Jimmy and Freddie Francis shiver outside Bray Studios during production of **Nightmare** *in January 1963.*

A sinister woman (Clytie Jessop) visits Janet (Jennie Linden) in her **Nightmare** (1964).

more drinking companion than friend, but, as in most things, he overdid that too and rather scared me off.

But, all in all, *Paranoiac* was a movie I would like to have been involved in much more than just as the screenwriter. And I *was* much more involved the next time I worked with Freddie Francis.

Nightmare was my fourth psycho-type drama for Hammer and once again the whole thing revolved around a pretty girl in dire peril. This time she was played by Jennie Linden. The part was supposed to have been played by Julie Christie, at that time a struggling newcomer. We had already cast her and she'd signed the contract when we got a call from her agent. Please will we release her, she's got the offer of a better job. Naturally enough we said no. Then Julie herself called. Please! Please! Okay. What was the better job? It seemed a movie had started shooting two weeks before and now the producers wanted to change the leading lady. The girl they'd signed and filmed with so far was not very good. Biting the bullet all round, they decided to start the movie over, hopefully with the girl who had been second in the running for the part.

Julie was practically in tears, so Freddie and I eventually told her we'd release her. She went off to do *Billy Liar*, John Schlesinger's first feature, which turned out to be one of the seminal movies of the sixties. Even Freddie and I admit that movie did more for her career than *Nightmare* would have done. This is not to denigrate Jennie Linden's efforts. She was vulnerable, pretty, and gave a thoroughly competent performance.

But, like I said, the original storyline was starting to fray a little round the edges by now. Janet (Jennnie Linden) is mentally unbalanced by a recurring nightmare about her mother, whom she saw stab her father to death six years earlier. A teacher at Janet's boarding school, Mary (Brenda Bruce), arranges to accompany her home for a few days. There they meet Grace (Moira Redmond), who has been hired by Janet's legal guardian, Henry Baxter (David Knight), to be her 'companion'. Janet starts to be haunted by a tall, ghostly woman she's never seen before, finding her stabbed on a couple of occasions. The local doctor tells Henry that Janet is in desperate need of psychiatric help.

After another nightmare, Janet makes a suicide attempt. Later, she meets Henry's wife for the first time... it's the ghostly woman who has been haunting her. She breaks down and stabs the woman to death. Grace, wearing a mask resembling Mrs Baxter, is revealed to be the ghost. The whole thing has turned out to be an elaborate plan by Henry and Grace to get rid of his wife. Janet is carted off to the asylum and three months later Henry and Grace, married now, move into the house. A string of events occur which make Grace think Henry is cheating on her and eventually, in a fit of fury, she stabs him to death. It is Mary and the faithful old chauffeur (George A Cooper), plus housekeeper Mrs Gibbs (Irene Richmond), who planned the denouement when they discovered what Henry and Grace had really done.

Having re-read what I've just written, I can only say it was just as well I didn't try to sell it based on the storyline. Especially with the dreadful title somebody foisted on it (not me): *Here's the Knife Dear – Now Use It*.

A bit like telling the entire story in one line. Without the full treatment which I presented, it would never have got made. But it did get made and it turned out quite well. An interesting point in the structure of the story is that it deals with two separate cases of a woman being driven to commit a mad act, first Janet, then Grace. Once Janet was carried off to the asylum, about two thirds of the way through the movie, we never see her again.

The actual shooting went very smoothly. Locations were done at Oakley Court in six inches of snow, which was a bitch to shoot but looked very good. The studio work was done, of course, at Bray. Bernie Robinson again, assisted by art director Don Mingaye, gave us his usual beautifully designed, understated sets which were well photographed by a new man at Bray, John Wilcox. But the main thing I remember is what a joy to work with Freddie was. Producing a movie can be very hard work, especially if the director is too demanding. Maybe he wants a crane when he doesn't really need

Janet (Jennie Linden) is trapped in the asylum in **Nightmare** (1964).

one; maybe he says something must be shot on night location rather than day for night; maybe he wants this, that or the other. Whatever, some directors will dig in their heels and tell you that's the way it's going to be, or else! Leslie Norman was like that. Freddie wasn't.

'Can we afford it?' he'd ask. Invariably I'd tell him we couldn't. So he'd make do another way. Maybe he bitched about it when he got home, but I don't remember him and me ever falling out.

Freddie got some nice press for *Nightmare* too. 'Francis can be welcomed to the short roll of British horror specialists' (the *Times*). 'Slick and smooth' (the *Observer*). On the other hand the *New York Times* said it was 'a cardboard fake' and *Films and Filming* called it 'a routine exercise.'

But they hadn't seen nothing yet. The next up for Freddie and I was *Hysteria*. Before that he'd done one more for Hammer, *The Evil of Frankenstein*, which I had nothing to do with, probably because I was busy writing *Hysteria*. Or maybe Tony and/or Michael had decided that I'd done as much Gothic horror as they wanted from me. So Tony wrote it under his pen name John Elder. I never saw the movie, but Tom Johnson in his Hammer book says that '*The Evil of Frankenstein* is an example of what can go wrong when a film company abandons what it does best, and it shows how important Terry Fisher and Jimmy Sangster were to Hammer's success.' No harm in blowing one's own trumpet now and then.

I remember *Nightmare* as being a fun movie to make. No major hitches, no prima donnas in the cast or crew, a slip and a slide in the schedule every now and then, usually pulled back a couple of days later. But *Hysteria*? Forget it! Not a happy experience at all.

First, we made the movie at MGM Studios in Borehamwood. That was okay, but it meant that we didn't have the regular Hammer crew around us. Not that I'm complaining about the crew we *did* have, but it just wasn't the same. Second, the lead was played by an American, Robert Webber. He was a very good actor who had never become a star but was always working. You might not remember the name but you'd recognise the face straight away. He was the guy who never got the girl, the hero's best friend, the fourth man at the poker table... you name it, he'd played it.

The female lead was an actress named Lelia Goldoni, who was a comparative newcomer to the business. She wasn't a bad actress, but then she wasn't all that good either. Webber, who had worked with top Hollywood people, took an instant dislike to her and proceeded to put her down whenever he got the chance. This destroyed what little confidence she had and affected her performance. Not that there was

Mr Smith (Robert Webber) doubts his own sanity in **Hysteria** *(1965).*

Robert Webber, Jennifer Jayne, Lelia Goldoni, Maurice Denham, Anthony Newlands and Irene Richmond in **Hysteria** *(1965).*

CLASSIC SCENE

 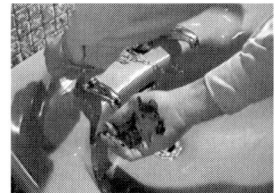 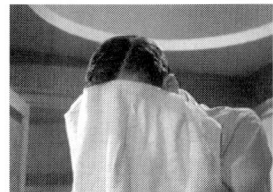 

HYSTERIA

My favourite scene here is the one where Smith (Webber) is washing his hands in the bathroom basin, when he closes the mirror over the basin and reveals, standing behind him, the woman who has been haunting him, Denise (Goldoni). The shock of seeing her suddenly outweighs the fact there is no apparent threat in the scene. This is almost entirely due to the way that Freddie Francis shot it.

  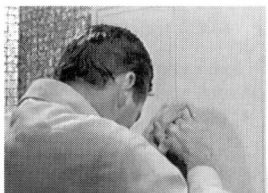 

much of a performance for her to give, because the part, as with most of the others, was strictly to formula.

The Robert Webber character is being treated for amnesia after a car crash in which the driver who was giving him a lift was killed. Because he can't remember a thing, he's given the name Mr Smith. He is unaware of who is paying for his medical treatment and the apartment he is using. The only clue is a photograph of a beautiful woman torn from a magazine. Smith hires a private investigator (Maurice Denham) to help him in his search for his past life. At the same time, he starts to hear strange noises in his apartment. Then he learns that the woman in the photograph was murdered a few months earlier. Later, the woman (Lelia Goldoni) turns up in his apartment claiming to be the widow of the driver who was killed in the accident. He later discovers a woman's body in the shower, but by this time, unknown to us, he has regained his memory. He tricks his psychiatrist (Anthony Newlands) and the Lelia Goldoni character into confessing their plan to frame him for the murder of Newlands' wife.

The script was very much the mixture as before, something I was beginning to get rather fed up with. And I think it showed. Hammer, it seems, had also had enough for the time being. This was the last of this particular cycle of movies until a double-bill in the early seventies, *Straight on Till Morning* and *Fear in the Night*.

But, even with as weak a script as this, I think the finished product could have been better. The main problem was the casting of Webber. He was far too powerful a character for one to believe that he was going insane. Jennifer Jayne and Anthony Newlands trailed along and Maurice Denham did his best with an over-the-top private investigator part. As for Lelia Goldoni, the poor girl didn't stand a chance.

Add all these rather depressing ingredients together and the whole piece justly deserved the bad reviews it got. 'Producer-writer Jimmy Sangster has been caught here in a web of his own cleverness' from the *Kinematograph Weekly*. While the *New York Times* decided that 'Bland lethargy ruined a decent plot.'

I disagree. Even the plot wasn't all that decent.

CHAPTER 12

The Pirates of Blood River
The Devil-Ship Pirates
The Terror of the Tongs

THE PIRATES OF BLOOD RIVER
(filmed 3 July to 31 August 1961,
released 13 July 1962)

THE DEVIL-SHIP PIRATES
(filmed 19 August to 4 October 1963,
released 9 August 1964)

THE TERROR OF THE TONGS
(filmed 19 April to 30 May 1960,
released 29 September 1961)

Now we come to what I call the 'tits and swords' movies that Hammer started to produce. I'd written one already for Bob Baker and Monty Berman of Tempean Films called *The Hellfire Club*. Michael Carreras and I, with our families, were cavorting by a swimming pool one Sunday afternoon when he asked me if I'd be interested in writing a pirate movie. Sure I'd be interested, I told him. There's one small problem, he went on. Hammer can't afford a boat. A pirate movie without a boat? Like Robin Hood without bows and arrows. Still, I told him I'd have a go. The result was *The Pirates of Blood River*.

I've always been a fan of the 'desperate hours'-type movie where a gang of villains hole up somewhere taking the legitimate occupants as hostages while they plan and execute their crime and make their getaway. One of the standard suspense plot lines. So why not try it with pirates?

Jonathan Standing (Kerwin Mathews), the son of the leader of a Huguenot settlement in the Caribbean, is banished to a penal colony by his father Jason (Andrew Keir), charged with adultery. He eventually escapes from the prison and is taken in by a band of pirates led by LaRoche (Christopher Lee), who is convinced that the colony has a cache of gold hidden somewhere. La Roche tells Jonathan that if he is taken to the colony, he will restore law and order there. Jonathan believes him and leads him to the colony where he and his men start behaving like the pirates they are, raping and killing. They threaten to destroy the whole village unless they are told where the gold is hidden.

La Roche eventually discovers that a huge statue of the colony's founder is solid gold. He takes it and, with Jonathan and his father as hostages, starts back to his ship. Led by Henry (Glenn Corbett), Jason's other son and Jonathan's brother, the islanders pick off the pirates one by one through clever ambushes. Mac (Michael Ripper), one of the pirates, leads a mutiny against LaRoche and, with the statue tied to a raft, tries to make it back to the ship. The boat sinks and the pirates are devoured by piranhas. Meanwhile Jonathan has killed La Roche in a duel.

And there you have it. A pirate picture with no boats.

I wrote a full shooting script where I originally called the Chris Lee character Captain Doom. I described him as:

...a strange and fascinating creature. But the fascination is evil. At first glance he might be called handsome. The bone structure of his face

*Christopher Lee as the ruthless LaRoche in **The Pirates of Blood River** (1962).*

is good. But there is a strange emptiness about it, for it is the face of a man without a heart. DOOM has wit, intelligence, energy... even a sense of humour. But where his heart should be is a piece of ice... or nothing. DOOM's whole appearance and the way he moves is so elegant that it is some moments before we notice that he is a cripple. His left arm is badly withered, bent at the elbow and held close against his body. His hand, with fingers crooked upwards, is like an upturned claw.

With a description like that, Christopher Lee was guaranteed to get the part.

But somewhere down the line, long before shooting started, the powers that be decided that my script needed to be rewritten. I never did find out which 'powers that be' they were, but it was probably Mike Frankovich, the head of Columbia in England at the time, an amiable man who knew the business inside out. The rewrites refined to some extent the cold-blooded evil that was Captain Doom. He was re-christened La Roche, and while remaining a cripple, he was given more depth of character than I originally wrote for him. They didn't ask me to do the rewrites, probably because I was long gone on some other project. Instead, they were done by John Hunter, whom I never met, and by the director, John Gilling, who I knew from other projects.

The final script, according to the onscreen credits, was merely based on my storyline. Obviously I wasn't particularly concerned about this at the time or I

would have screamed blue bloody murder. In America, where I worked later, it would automatically have gone to Writers Guild arbitration, and they would have decided how the 'on screen' titles should have been. Whereas here, at least in those days, there was no such provision. In fact, on reflection, I'm not even sure I was aware of the credit change because for years afterwards I claimed this movie in various cv's and credit lists as 'Original Screenplay by Jimmy Sangster'. Obviously I didn't go to see the movie when it came out or I'd have spotted the credit change then. I'm afraid to admit it was often the case I didn't go to see the movie. Some I've not seen to this day.

What they didn't change to any great extent was the character of Jason Standing, played by Andrew Keir. I described him as:

...the crumbling shell of a man consumed by the inward fires of religious mania. Other Elders of the settlement like MARTIN and MASON are hard-faced men of a coarser stamp. Elders, like STANDING, they appear less important and impressive. But, in fact, forming a cabal with the two other Elders of the governing body, they make the decisions and wield the real power in the community. STANDING, the unassailable patriarch, is merely a righteous figurehead behind whom the unrighteous operate. With him at their head they have been able to estab-lish a kind of religious dictatorship, a holy reign of terror.

...all good, meaty stuff.

The whole cast was first rate, as usual in a Hammer film. Kerwin Mathews, who went on to do *Maniac* for me, was suitably swashbuckling. Christopher gave his usual energetic, menacing, first-rate performance and dear old Michael Ripper was given a part he could get his teeth into. Oliver Reed was there, so too was Glenn Corbett, an American who lent virtually nothing to the box office and very little to the part.

The finished product was well-received. *Kine Weekly* described it as 'Thrilling story, robust charac-terisation, hectic highlights.' Unusually for a Hammer film, it received a 'U' certificate from the

The Pirates of Blood River *premièred at the London Pavilion on 13 July 1962.*

Christopher Lee and dapper producer Anthony Nelson Keys during production of **The Devil-Ship Pirates** *at Bray Studios in autumn 1963.*

censor and, as part of a double-bill, it did very well at the box office. So well, in fact, that Hammer decided maybe they'd do another pirate picture. This one was called *The Devil-Ship Pirates* and this time they said I could have a boat.

Once again I used the 'desperate hours' syndrome. The *Diablo*, a pirate ship under the command of Captain Robeles (Christopher Lee) has been commissioned to serve with the Spanish Armada. The ship is badly damaged and Captain Robeles orders the crew to break off the battle and run for it, much to the horror of a young officer of the Spanish navy, Manuel (Barry Warren). Eventually the ship is grounded in marshland off the Cornish coast

where they hope to make the repairs necessary for them to return to Spain. Then they discover that they are close to a small isolated village where Manuel informs the population that, in fact, the Spaniards defeated the English in the sea battle and now occupy the country.

The pirate crew take over the village and order the villagers to start repairing the ship. But the local blacksmith, Tom (Andrew Keir), and his son, Harry (John Cairney), are suspicious. They smuggle a young boy out of town to go to the next village for help and information, while Harry goes to the beached Diablo looking for his sister, who is a prisoner on board. Captain Robeles is invited to stay at the manor house

Filming the scene in which Captain Robeles (Christopher Lee), Pepe (Michael Ripper) and the crew of the Diablo row ashore in **The Devil-Ship Pirates** *(1964).*

by Sir Basil Smeeton (Ernest Clark). Meanwhile, Manuel learns that the pirates don't intend to return to Spain but to go back to their original occupation, namely piracy on the high seas. Harry finally rescues Jane (Natasha Pyne) from the Diablo and she returns to the village where she tells the villagers the truth, namely that the English won the great sea battle and the Spanish Armada was routed.

Harry and Tom begin to gather arms, but Sir Basil betrays them and Tom is hanged in front of the whole village. The pirates use the villagers to repair the Diablo, ready for sailing on the next high tide. When Robeles announces that he is going to take half-a-dozen of the village women as hostages, Harry and Manuel, who has now switched sides, rig the ship

with gunpowder. A fire is started and they rescue the hostages, but Manuel is badly wounded. Robeles and Harry fight and, at the last moment, when it looks like Robeles will gain the upper hand, Manuel pulls himself together sufficiently to shoot Robeles. Harry abandons the ship, which eventually blows up.

All this was a bit 'the mixture as before'. But, in the long run, most of my movies were. If it ain't broke why fix it? This time it was Don Sharp who was hired to direct. He'd just done *The Kiss of the Vampire* for Hammer and they were very pleased with the results. Where *Kiss* had been Don's first Gothic horror, this was the first time he swashed a buckle. For him, the first problem was to get in all the quite violent and grisly action and still manage to get a 'U' certificate, which Hammer insisted on. But he managed admirably. His second problem was the old Hammer one of budget restrictions. 'Make it good but make it cheap.' Again he succeeded, thanks to the Bray crew.

As far as the *Diablo* was concerned, up front I was told we could have a boat as long as it didn't have to actually float. Bernie Robinson designed it and Arthur Banks, who'd been a plasterer when I first joined Hammer and who was now head of construction at Bray, built the ship at the studio at a cost of around £17,000. It was built on old army pontoons which had seen better days. Finally, when the time came to launch it in the local water-filled sand and gravel pit, the two cranes couldn't handle the weight and an extra one had to be brought in. Eventually, they got it secured solidly to firm ground. Except – something that they didn't find out until later – the bottom of a gravel pit isn't firm ground, it shifts. After that the rigging and sails were fitted.

Ian Scoones, a special effects expert who worked for Les Bowie, was in charge of the whole thing and he tells the story about Hammer hiring somebody who was supposed to know about boats to keep an eye on the set while it was being used. Apparently he was something of a drinking man and the production crew would keep him tanked up so he would stay off their backs. He'd go around all day saying 'This boat's gonna sink. We're all doomed. We're all going to drown.' He was damn near right. One day, the tea-break boat came out from the shore and the whole cast and crew ran to the side of the ship, which promptly tilted over and dumped everyone into the water.

But it was a first-class set which Hammer hoped eventually to rent out to other production companies, but by the end of production they figured too much damage had been done to her and so, instead of using a model, they used the actual set to stage the final fire and explosions. And very impressive it was too.

In fact, the whole movie was quite impressive. Once again the performances were up to standard. Andrew Keir, this time a hero; Michael Ripper, as always; and Christopher, wielding a sword and dagger impressively. But, more than that, Hammer had by now become extremely adept at making a silk purse out of a sow's ear. Unlike today, nobody in the crew

Christopher Lee swashes his buckle aboard the Diablo *in* **The Devil-Ship Pirates** *(1964). The watching crew-members were wise to stay on dry land.*

Christopher Lee as Chung King in **The Terror of the Tongs** *(1961). The role predated his better-known portrayal of Fu Manchu.*

and/or cast was overpaid; every penny spent was up there on the screen. This was one of the cornerstones of Hammer's success during the sixties. The film looked as if it had cost five times what it actually did.

The pre-title sequence, the great sea battle, was, of course, shot with models, also supervised by Scoones. Maybe the sequence looked a bit foggier than it should, but that was because in the background they were building the motorway which became the M4, and lots of smoke was the only way to mask it.

My criticisms of the finished product are all minor except for one. And that one was my fault as much as anyone else's. The picture opens with a Spanish crew all speaking English, which they continue to do throughtout the movie. This would have been okay if the whole picture had taken place in Spain. But with the villagers all being English, the crew all Spanish, chatting away to each other, I think we got away with murder. Still, I don't see how else we could have done it.

The critics liked the movie. 'Sturdy, swashbuckling adventure, soberly scripted and acted but with thrills ample and action well staged' (*Daily Cinema*) and, from America, 'Impressively mounted adventure meller' (*Variety*).

I should have been so lucky on another movie I wrote for Hammer a couple of years before either of the pirate movies. *The Terror of the Tongs*. Bernie Robinson had built a great set on the lot at Bray for a movie called *Visa to Canton*. It represented a large merchant ship moored dockside in some oriental port. It was very impressive and, for Hammer, very expensive. They decided they had to use it in their next picture. That way, they could split the cost of the set over two budgets. Good business. Except they didn't have anything to shoot that required a Chinese dockside. So they came to me and asked me if I could help out. I must have needed the money, because I told them I'd come to their rescue and I wrote *The Terror of the Tongs*.

Opening paragraph...

Hong Kong, 1910. A bustling, growing city. But hidden deep amongst its teeming thousands was an organisation that thrived on vice, terror and corruption. The Red Dragon Tong.

I ask you, with a premise like that, who could go wrong? Or so I thought as I wrote the script.

The Hong Kong waterfront is held in a grip of terror by the Red Dragon Tong, who profit from white slave-trading and drug trafficking, led by the ruthless Chung King (Christopher Lee). A 16-year-old girl, Helena, is killed by Chung King's men when she accidentally comes across a list naming all the Red Dragon's top agents. Her father, Captain Jackson (Geoffrey Toone), vows to track down her killers. He eventually catches a Red Dragon money collector and

楼國中新區 沙沙 新中 中

HAMMER FILM PRODUCTIONS
invite you to

A
CHINESE BARBECUE

on the River Bank
at
BRAY STUDIOS
WINDSOR

ON WEDNESDAY, MAY 18, 1960
12 NOON-3 PM

Classic Scene

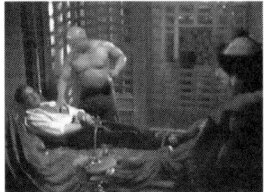 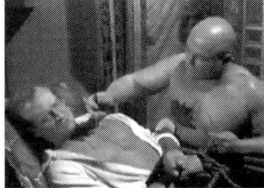 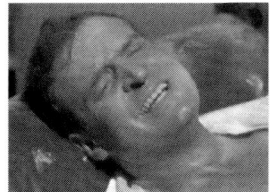 

The Terror of the Tongs

I suppose my favourite scene has to be the one where the hero is tortured by having the marrow of his bones scraped. Heaven only knows where I came up with that one. I'd like to think I read about it somewhere, but I have a sneaky feeling I made it all up myself.

While it doesn't come under the 'classic scene' heading, I'd like to say that Christopher Lee's performance in this movie was really excellent whereas Yvonne Monlaur's was quite dreadful. As for the rest of the cast, they were just about okay. While the director, Anthony Bushell, must take some of the blame for this, I too must take my share. If the lines aren't there, you can't play them.

 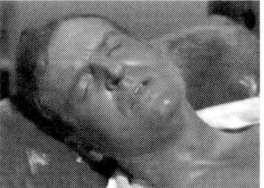  

beats him until he tells him all he wants to know. The money lender's wife, Lee (Yvonne Monlaur), joins Jackson in his quest.

Eventually Jackson is captured and taken to the Tong headquarters where he is tortured by having his bones scraped. He manages to escape. Chung King must now kill Jackson to save face and he arranges to lure him to the wharf where he is to be murdered in a 'ceremonial killing'. Lee intervenes and is killed by a hatchetman. The dockworkers realise that the Tong secret is broken and assist the anti-Tong police agents in an assault on the Tong headquarters. As his organisation is destroyed, Chung King chooses to die at the hands of his own executioner.

I can only quote Tom Johnson here. 'The Terror of the Tongs was a nasty entry in Hammer's move from Gothic horror to costume adventure.' I hate to admit it, but he's right. And I'm partly to blame. The old adage that you can't make a good movie from a bad script is amply demonstrated here. On the other hand, I don't think the assembled company would have made a much better movie even if the script had been good. Apart from the line producer, Ken Hyman, I don't think anybody was too sure what they were doing. As for Ken, he eventually left Hammer and went on to produce The Hill and The Dirty Dozen, before going to Hollywood to head up production at Warner Bros and later MGM.

A copy of this movie is almost impossible to find these days but I was able to run a copy during my research for this book. I'd rather I hadn't because I'd begun to think I was knocking it too much. Unfortunately, I wasn't. It was just as bad as I'd feared. But I have to admit, at the time, I didn't lose any sleep over it. I don't think the powers that be at Hammer did either. Or if they did, they didn't blame me because I went on working for them, on and off, for the next 12 years.

CHAPTER 13

The Nanny

THE NANNY
(filmed 5 April to 3 June 1965, released 7 October 1965)

*T*he Nanny was originally a novel by Evelyn Piper. I never met Ms Piper but I'm eternally grateful to her for writing the book. Hammer bought the film rights and turned it over to me to write the screenplay on the basis that if they managed to get it going, and if I was interested, then I could produce it too. I think they were hoping I'd turn it into one of my psycho-type horror movies. But, as I mentioned earlier, that type of picture had pretty much run its course as far as I was concerned. Also, to my mind, the subject matter didn't slot easily into that style of movie.

The story was pretty straightforward. After two years of psychiatric treatment, ten-year-old Joey Fane (William Dix) comes home to his parents, Bill and Virgie Fane (James Villiers and Wendy Craig). They believe he is suffering from a massive guilt complex due to the accidental drowning of his baby sister, Susy, in the bath two years before. Virgie confides to her trusted Nanny (Bette Davis) that she is frightened of the boy and doesn't feel she can cope with him after what he has done. She herself is neurotic in the extreme, behaving like a child, a state of affairs which Nanny encourages. She's not helped by her indifferent husband, a Queen's Messenger who's away from home most of the time.

When Bill and Nanny arrive at the 'school' to pick Joey up, the doctor (Maurice Denham) admits that Joey might still have some psychological problems.

Joey refuses to speak to Nanny or have any contact with her. He also refuses to sleep in the bedroom that has been prepared for him or eat anything that Nanny cooks. Virgie goes down with food poisoning and is taken to hospital and Joey is accused of poisoning her. He remains adamant that it's Nanny who is the guilty party. As Bill is away, Virgie's sister Pen (Jill Bennett), who suffers from a weak heart, is called in to stay the night as Joey refuses to stay in the place alone with Nanny. She is dismayed when Joey makes Nanny swear not to come into the bathroom while he is taking a bath. Then, later, she is woken from a nap by a soaking and frantic Joey who swears Nanny just tried to drown him. The distress brings on an angina attack and Nanny fetches her medication.

Meanwhile, Joey visits his new-found friend Bobby (Pamela Franklin), the daughter of the doctor who lives in the apartment above. He tells her that Nanny tried to kill him. He tells her the events surrounding his baby sister's death two years earlier where we see, in flashback, Nanny called out of the house when she is supposed to be minding the two of them. Susy tries to bath her doll, but falls into the bathtub and knocks herself out. Nanny returns, goes to the bathroom and turns on the taps without seeing Susy. When she returns, she discovers Susie's drowned body and, unable to accept the fact, she starts to bath the dead Susie. Joey sees her and picks up the phone to call for help, but Nanny grabs him, threatening to bath him too. When the authorities are called, Nanny tells them that Joey was responsible for the death.

Nanny (Bette Davis) keeps Penelope's (Jill Bennett) life-saving drugs out of reach. One of the most disturbing scenes from **The Nanny** *(1965).*

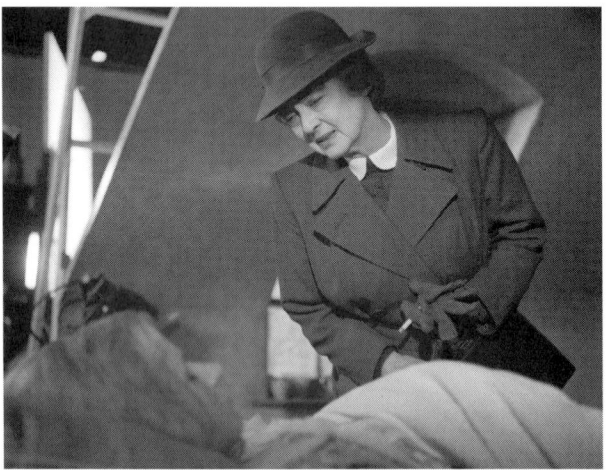

*Nanny (Bette Davis) discovers the body of her estranged daughter Janet in this rehearsal shot from **The Nanny** (1965).*

*Dr Wills (Alfred Burke) admonishes the distraught Nanny (Bette Davis) in **The Nanny** (1965).*

Now, out of flashback, Pen sees Nanny lurking suspiciously outside Joey's bedroom door. She confronts Nanny and suffers a heart attack while struggling with her. Nanny refuses to fetch her medication and, while Pen dies, she tells her side of the story. How, two years ago, the day she left the children alone, she had a call from a doctor to tell her that her own daughter, who was given away at six months old, had died having an abortion. The doctor blames the daughter's life of sadness and neglect on Nanny, who has always been too busy looking after other people's children.

Now, with Pen dead, Nanny forces her way into Joey's room, where she knocks him unconscious and places him in the bathtub, holding his head under water. At this moment she hallucinates and sees Susy's body in the bath and she realises the horror of what she has done. She pulls Joey out of the tub and he bolts. She goes to her room and starts to pack. Her life is over. Later, Joey is reunited with his mother in hospital.

As you can see, hardly the basis for a psycho-type horror movie. So I wrote it as I saw it, namely a first-class psychological thriller in which, while we might end up with a couple of bodies, namely Susy and Pen, nobody actually takes a knife or a gun to anyone.

Once the first draft of the script was ready, it got an immediate go-ahead from the American powers that be who, at that time consisted of Seven Arts and

20th Century-Fox. Next up, the cast. And while we're involved with the casting, let's look around for a director. Check availability and salary. But don't sign him up yet. Unlike earlier Hammer movies, we weren't going to get a director on board before we cast the lead part. We were looking for a 'name', and 'names' invariably have director approval.

The name everyone seemed excited about was Greer Garson, a movie star from the old school. *Mrs Miniver*. Mrs Chips. *Madame Curie*. Seven times nominated for the best actress Academy Award, winning it for *Mrs Miniver*. Seven Arts forwarded a copy of the script to her, she read it and while she didn't say no, she didn't say yes either. First she'd like to meet the writer/producer.

She had houses in New York and Los Angeles, but she didn't want to meet me in either of those places. Please would I visit her in Santa Fe, New Mexico, where her husband, Buddy Fogelson, who I believe was in oil, owned a spread called the Forked Lightning Ranch. It was a long drag, but what the hell? Even if I didn't think she was right for the movie, I was being well paid. So I packed a bag and flew to New York and then on to Santa Fe. I was met at the airport by Mr and Mrs Buddy Fogelson, and a charming couple they were. She was every bit as elegant as I remembered her on screen and he was a delightful man who was obviously enormously proud of his movie star wife. They drove me a few miles out of town to their ranch, where I was shown to my room and told that, after a wash and brush-up, I was expected for afternoon tea on the lawn. And, out there, on the edge of the New Mexico desert, that's what we had, a thoroughly English tea, complete with crumpets and a silver tea service.

That night we went to a restaurant in Santa Fe where we were treated like royalty, which the Fogelsons represented in that part of the world. They owned this huge spread, she was on the board of the University and they had financed a couple of buildings on campus. Big wheels, charming people.

The following morning we went through the script briefly. She was polite, said she liked it but was a little worried about what it might do to her 'image'. I didn't like to mention it but, as far as the current cinema audience was concerned, she no longer had one. It was a long time since she had made a movie. They loaned me a stetson and a pair of cowboy boots and, after a picnic lunch somewhere out on the range or the prairie or whatever they called it, I was driven to the airport where I caught a plane back to London.

During the flight, I thought long and hard. Yes, she was a wonderful actress and yes, she was (or had been) a big star and yes, she was a charming lady. But as the Nanny? No way. So I told them at Hammer that I thought Greer Garson was wrong for the part. They weren't impressed. As far as they were concerned, if Greer Garson wanted the part, then she'd got it, whatever the writer/producer might have to say. A couple of weeks later we got a message from Los Angeles. Sorry, Greer Garson doesn't want to do the movie. How about Bette Davis? Now they were talking.

We'd already pencilled in Seth Holt to direct but Miss Davis had, of course, 'director approval'. So Seth and I duly flew to Los Angeles where Seven Arts had booked us into the largest suite you've ever seen at the magnificent Bel Air Hotel on Stone Canyon. Bette was living in a small house further down the canyon at that time. The morning after we arrived we walked a few hundred yards down the road, rang the front doorbell of an extremely modest little house and madam herself answered the door. We were asked in, we introduced ourselves. We were offered a cup of tea, which she made herself, and then we were duly auditioned. At least, Seth was auditioned. I just sat there.

What did he think of this picture and that performance? Did he agree that William Wyler was one of the best directors of all time? What was his opinion of *Whatever Happened to Baby Jane?* In *The Nanny*, how would he handle the scene where so and so does such and such? And, dragging me into the discussion, didn't we think the penultimate scenes were a bit over the top? Impressive stuff to someone who was used to having actors who, when offered a part, asked 'When does shooting start? How much do I get paid? Oh, and maybe I could have a look at the script.'

After half an hour we went back to the hotel. As far as I was concerned, that was it. The following day I caught a plane back to London, leaving Seth in Hollywood to get drunk with some old buddies he hadn't seen for some time. Five days later we get a call. Miss Davis would be happy to accept Seth Holt as director. 'When does shooting start? How much do I get paid? Oh, and I'd like a couple of changes to the script...'

We went about the rest of the casting. None of it was a problem except the part of the young boy, Joey. He had to be a very good actor, and at the age of ten they're quite thin on the ground. After 15 or more auditions, we finally got to meet William Dix. Instant success, as far as we were concerned. He looked good and he read for the part beautifully. The remainder of the casting was comparatively easy. English stalwarts all of them, except for the enchanting little baby girl who played Susy, Angharad Aubrey. Where she came from or where she went to, I know not.

As the movie was partly financed by British distributor ABPC, we shot it at their studio in Borehamwood. Bray was busy, so we were unable to get Bernie Robinson to do the sets, so we used Edward Carrick, who had handled production deseign on *Hysteria* for me. I say 'sets' when, apart from one dingy little backstreet bedroom, there was only one other. This was a large composite set of the Fane apartment, three bedrooms, living room, dining room, kitchen, bathroom, huge entrance hall and an outdoor, first floor terrace. There was also the outside corridor leading to an elevator. The cinematographer was Harry Waxman, a first time for me. Nice guy, good cameraman.

CLASSIC SCENE

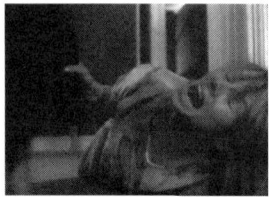

THE NANNY

*O*ne of the classic scenes in this movie has to be the death of Pen (Jill Bennett). This is the first time we fully understand the true evil of Nanny. It is extremely well played, especially by Bette Davis who watches Pen die with a suitably sorrowful, pitying expression.

The subsequent flashback breaks away from the scene and, when we return, the face of the dead Pen is a shock in spite of the fact that her death was inevitable. Seth Holt directed this sequence in such a way as to get the maximum impact with minimum histrionics.

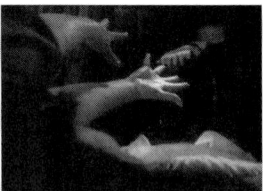

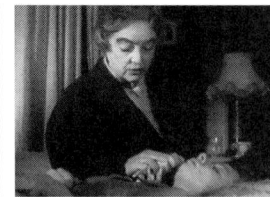

Around two weeks before the start of shooting, Bette Davis arrived in England. She came in on one of the ocean-going *Queens*. Seth and I drove down to Southampton to meet her. We had rented for her a huge house in Elstree quite close to the studios. She was accompanied by her son, around ten years old, and a rather strange lady companion/gofer-type person named Violla Rubber. Contrary to what you might imagine, she never had a 'great entourage'. One person was provided for in her contract, and that's what she had. Violla Rubber on this, the first movie I made with her, and some delightful middle-aged guy whose name I've forgotten on the second.

There were a certain amount of wardrobe problems before we started. Bette insisted that we buy the Nanny's uniforms at a 'nanny's uniform shop.' Authenticity was high on her agenda. So we ordered various sizes and they were delivered to her at her house. She decided that none of them fitted so my au pair girl, Denise, took time off from minding my son

to go to work with a needle and thread. I'm not sure why the wardrobe mistress, Mary Gibson, didn't do it. It was too early in the picture for Bette to have taken a dislike to her. A couple of days before the start of shooting, we had a script read-through which went well, and the next Monday, we were off and running.

I've read something that Seth Holt wrote about the picture. 'Davis got flu during shooting, and sometimes she'd stay away altogether, holding up shooting while she sent in day-to-day reports on her condition.' Well, if memory serves me correctly, Bette didn't have one single day away during shooting. If she had, we wouldn't have finished on schedule, which we did with a little time to spare.

Tough. Demanding. A perfectionist. She was all these things. Awkward bitch too, on occasions. But she never asked for anything that she didn't consider was to the benefit of the movie as a whole. If it could be proved to her otherwise, fine, she'd withdraw her demand.

She would invariably preface a request with the phrase 'I've starred in 62 movies and...' It's difficult to argue with somebody who has been nominated for an Academy Award ten times and won it twice. You've got to believe they know what they're talking about.

On the first day of shooting there was a bedroom scene between her and Wendy Craig. Wendy is in bed and Bette is sitting on the side of the bed talking to her. As usual, Seth filmed the two-shot first and then went in for the close-ups. Wendy first, because to shoot Bette's we had to pull out the back of the set and bring in a false ceiling, maybe 20 minutes' work. After work was over for the day I get a call in my office. Miss Davis would like a word in her dressing room. There she offered me a large drink before saying 'I have starred in... etc etc... and the director *always* does my close-up first.'

I explained about the work we had to do on the set before we could get round to her shot and I apologised for offending her, but it might happen again.

'You think I'm being an awkward bitch, don't you?' she said.

I did, but I didn't say so.

'Don't you understand that the person who does the first close-up controls the scene?'

I didn't. But later I thought about it. She was right.

A couple of other things bugged her. First was the fact that everybody could get a drink at lunchtime. In America, the studios are dry. In England they're not. She would scowl at the beer and wine on the tables where our people were eating lunch. Never mind that she invariably drunk herself legless after shooting finished. During the working day, zilch. Time-keeping was very important to her also. If the daily call sheet said 'Miss Davis on set at 9.30', she would be there, on the set at exactly 9.30. Nobody would have to call her from her dressing room or give her five minutes' warning. And God forbid the set wasn't ready for her when she turned up. It certainly kept the assistant director on his toes when he was making out the call sheet.

In fact, whatever Seth Holt might have recalled, shooting on this picture went pretty smoothly. Apart from Bette confiding in me one day that she thought Seth was 'a mountain of evil', she respected him as a director. In spite of what happened next, this turned out to be a good picture.

It could have been better. Seth had just finished supervising the director's cut when we got a call from the Fox offices in Soho Square, telling us that Seymour Poe, the head honcho of Fox's world-wide distribution, a very important person indeed, wanted

us to screen the picture for him. We explained there were no music or effects, no opticals and it was a pretty dirty print to boot. Not to worry, bring it over around 10.30 when Mr Poe and his good lady will take a look. Seth and I duly delivered the film and sat in the front row while Poe and his wife sat at the back. The screening finished and we looked back towards Poe, hopefully to take our bow.

'What happened to the ending?' he wanted to know.

The penultimate scene is when the Nanny character realises suddenly that she is in fact guilty of the crimes the little boy has been accusing her of all through the film. Riddled with guilt she goes to her room and starts to pack. Her life has finished. End of

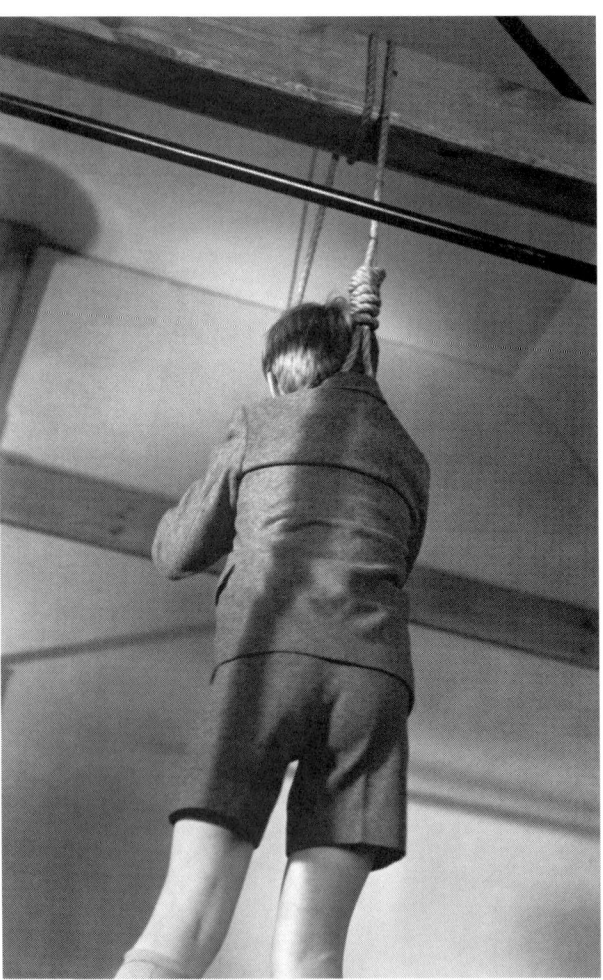

picture. At least, that was the end of the picture as written and as we had shot it. But not for Mr Poe. 'You can't end a movie that way. It's too downbeat. Have everybody leaving the theatre in a bad mood. Cheer 'em up, for Christ's sake. Give 'em a happy ending.'

We were forced to recall Wendy Craig and William Dix, rent studio space, build a set and spend two days shooting a new scene I had to write. A 'kiss, kiss, hug, hug, Nanny will get her just deserts' type scene. Much later, when Bette saw the movie in Los Angeles, she called me. She was furious. 'You shouldn't have let yourself be bullied that way', she said. 'You should have called me. I've starred in 62 movies and...'

That was Bette Davis professionally. Socially was a different matter altogether. She was a lonely and not very happy woman. It was essential for her to be the centre of attraction at any social gathering. If you behave badly enough, this isn't too hard. My wife Monica decided she'd like to give a dinner party for her at our house where she behaved so badly that Denise, our au pair girl, who was doubling as maid that evening, got so scared she dropped the coffee tray. One Friday night Monica and I managed to put together a small group and we went with Bette to Danny La Rue's nightclub. Just before the cabaret started a couple of the Beatles arrived. Bette said she was going to get their autographs for her daughter. She returned to our table a couple of minutes later almost apoplectic. 'Little bastards didn't know who I was,' she said. And she bitched about it loudly all through the cabaret, which she hated.

She could also be extremely intimidating. One day at the studio I got a call from comedian Frankie Howerd. I'd never met him but I was a great fan. He introduced himself before asking if he could possibly come down to the studio one day and have lunch with Bette Davis. No, he didn't know her, but he'd always worshipped her from afar. I checked with Bette who had never heard of him.

'What's he do?' she wanted to know.

I told her he was a comic, both stand-up and actor, an extremely funny man.

'At least we'll get a couple of laughs over lunch.'

'Gay?' she wanted to know.

'I've no idea,' said I.

'Take my word. He's gay. They adore me.' she said.

CLASSIC SCENE

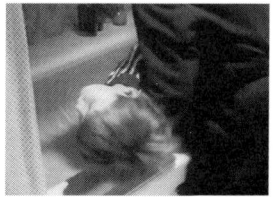   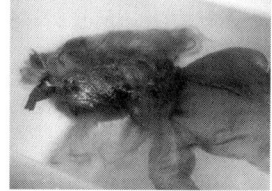

THE NANNY

A difficult choice. The first time we see Joey, hanging in the school dormitory, is a good one. So too is the scene in the bathroom where Nanny has her series of flashbacks cutting to the baby Susy alive, the baby Susy dead and the young Joey. In this sequence Seth Holt's talent as a great editor comes to the fore.

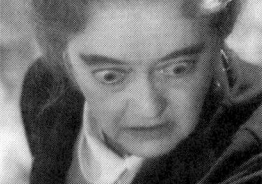 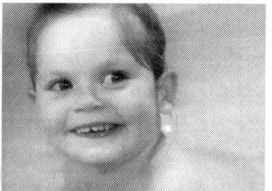 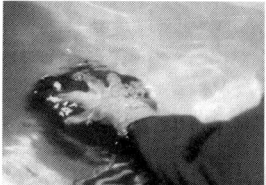 

Anyway, she agreed he could drop by for lunch, which he eventually did. Introductions were made, we ordered our food (no booze) and I sat back to enjoy the crosstalk between superstar and supercomic. Bette opened the dialogue.

'They tell me you're a comic,' she said. 'Make me laugh!'

Poor Frankie Howerd. He seized up completely. He managed to say about three words during the entire meal, and left before the coffee.

Also, somewhere down the line, Bette began to come on a little strong to me personally. I'd like to have said I was flattered, but I wasn't. It wasn't an easy situation to handle. She would take to calling me at home in the evening and asking me to come round to her place where she wanted to talk about the following day's work or bitch about what had happened today. I would duly drive the 35 minutes to her place where she would answer the front door herself, scotch on the rocks in hand, Violla and young son having been packed off to bed. She would have her say about the work problem, then she would ask me to have another drink and I would have to start ducking and diving.

I was desperately unoriginal in my evasion. 'I'd love to but I love my wife too much...' was my standard line. It worked. She respected the institution of marriage. At least she did until her next try.

Needless to say, I told Monica about this. She was very magnanimous about it. Not as difficult as it sounds, because Bette really wasn't very fanciable at that time. If I'd had Sigourney Weaver or Michelle Pfeiffer as my star, things may have turned out differently. But then neither of those two would have made a pass in the first place and I would have been far too chicken to have made the first move.

The day I put Bette on the plane home the Sangster household breathed a vast sigh of relief. Monica also said that if I ever did another movie with Bette, she was going to leave the country the day Bette arrived and not come back until I put her on the plane back to America. Not to worry, I told her. No way on God's green earth will I ever put myself through that again.

But, as I said earlier, all the aggro, inconvenience, whatever, was worth it. It was a good movie, one that I was proud to have been associated with.

CHAPTER 14

Dracula Prince of Darkness

DRACULA PRINCE OF DARKNESS
(filmed 26 April to 4 June 1965,
released 9 January 1966)

After the first *Dracula* movie, Hammer had asked me to do a screenplay for a sequel. This I did, calling it *Revenge of Dracula*. The mixture pretty much as before with Chris Lee and Peter Cushing reprising their original roles. Then, for reasons unknown to me at the time, they decided to go with *Brides* instead. That was okay with me. Another writing job, another pay day.

As for their reasons for shelving *Revenge* you can take your choice. One theory is the unavailability of Chris Lee, who had decided that now the Dracula part had made him a star, he didn't want to do it again. Another theory, in complete contrast, is that Hammer didn't, in fact, want Chris in the movie because they figured he wasn't a big enough star. This I don't go along with. A third theory is that they were worried how to bring Dracula back to life after the finale of the first movie where he dissolved into dust. I can't go along with that either. I'd brought Frankenstein back to life, what was the problem with Dracula? Anyway, I'd already worked it out in the script. The same resurrection as was to be used later in *Lust for a Vampire*, namely fresh blood onto ashes.

But, whatever the reason, my original script was shelved and Hammer went ahead with *Brides*. Now, six years later, they took *Revenge* out of the bottom drawer, dusted it off and gave it to me for a couple of rewrites and a polish. Get rid of Van Helsing and conjure up

another vampire hunter. I guess Peter Cushing was working elsewhere.

The movie opens with a pre-title sequence consisting of the finale of the first Hammer *Dracula* where the Count turns to dust. The stated reason for this was that we needed to give everyone's memory a jog as to what had gone before. But the real reason was that the first cut came up short on screentime and this was the cheapest way to add the extra few minutes needed. There was a problem in the different screen

Left: Christopher Lee, Barbara Shelley and Suzan Farmer in **Dracula Prince of Darkness**, *released in 1966.*

ratios, but this was solved by blurring the screen edges. Then they overlaid Andrew Keir's voice, telling the audience what was happening. It made a good opening, which was just as well, because it cost a lot of money. First, Hammer had to buy back the rights to the sequence from Universal, who now owned *Dracula*, and second, they had to pay Peter Cushing for his appearance. This they did by paying for the new roof he was having put on his house.

After the titles, the story opens in a small, mountainous Carpathian village where two English couples are in the middle of a vacation tour. They are Charles Kent (Francis Matthews), his wife Diana (Suzan Farmer), his brother Alan (Charles Tingwell) and Alan's wife Helen (Barbara Shelley). They meet Father Sandor (Andrew Keir), who warns them to avoid the

castle that lies near the village of Carlsbad. However, the following day they are stranded by their coachman at a lonely crossroads. A driverless coach appears and after they have clambered aboard, the uncontrollable horses deliver them at the castle.

There, Klove (Philip Latham), a weird-looking servant, tells them that his master has told him to always have the castle ready for travellers stranded in the area. They are wined and dined and eventually shown to their rooms. That night, Alan, wakened by a noise, follows Klove down to the crypt where Klove stabs him in the back and, suspending the body with a rope above a coffin filled with Dracula's ashes, cuts his throat. Alan's blood pours into the coffin and the ashes take the form of Count Dracula. (Boy, did we have battles with the censor over this sequence.) Next,

The undead Count (Christopher Lee) returns to haunt Castle Dracula in **Dracula Prince of Darkness**.

Klove lures Helen down to the crypt where she is seduced by Dracula. Stalked the next night by Dracula and the now-undead Helen, Charles and Diana ward off the vampires and escape in Klove's carriage. Sandor finds the terrified tourists after their carriage has crashed and takes them to his monastery.

But Dracula has traced them and is admitted to the monastery by mad Ludwig (Thorley Walters). At last I was able to include a Renfield-type character. He was the fly-eater in the original *Dracula* novel and over the years I'd received a lot of stick for leaving him out. But back to the story. Once in the monastery, Dracula gains access to Diana's room and is about to have her lick the blood from his chest (another battle with the censor) when Sandor and Charles arrive. Meanwhile Helen has been detained by some of the monks and, later, Charles is forced to look on in horror as she is staked by Sandor. Dracula escapes with Diana in a wagon driven by Klove. Sandor and Charles intercept the wagon and Charles shoots Klove. The wagon crashes and Dracula's coffin falls from it onto the frozen surface of the castle moat. Charles struggles with Dracula until Sandor recalls that running water is fatal to the undead. He directs his rifle fire at the ice around Dracula's feet. The ice gives way and, as Charles runs to safety, Dracula slips to his doom in the icy water.

Sounds like a good movie. All the well-tried Hammer ingredients and Christopher Lee finally reprising his role as the Count after eight years.

So why did I decide to call myself John Sansom on the titles? I asked for the pseudonym to be used because I was fed up with Gothic horror movies and felt that my career had moved well past this phase. It was a rewrite of something I'd done eight years earlier, a hangover from a time long gone. Since then, I'd done 'tits and swords,' both for Hammer and other companies; I'd done half-a-dozen of my psycho-type movies and I'd written and produced what I considered two of my best works, *Taste of Fear* and *The Nanny*. I'd already started to go to Los Angeles on various assignments; I just didn't want to step back to the time where my name once appeared on the billboard as *Jimmy (Frankenstein) Sangster*. So... Screenplay by John Sansom, from an idea by John Elder. Tony Hinds obviously didn't want his name on it either except as executive producer.

Some people claim that I used my pen name because I wasn't satisfied with the final movie. They're wrong on a couple of counts. Firstly I didn't even get to see the movie until it was ready for exhibition with the screen credits already in place and secondly I thought the final movie was pretty good. It had a good storyline, it was well shot, the characters were all well drawn and the cast did full justice to their parts. Terry Fisher directed in his usual competent fashion and Bernie Robinson and James Bernard provided the sets and musical score that had become expected of them. I mean, with that lot going for you, what's not to like?

Another point of controversy was why Dracula didn't have any lines. In the previous movie, the first

Dracula, he had half-a-dozen lines at the beginning of the movie when he introduces himself to Jonathan Harker. He needed those lines because nobody knew he was a vampire at that time. Once his true colours were revealed he never opened his mouth again, except to suck blood. This time, we know exactly who he is when he first appears. He is Count Dracula, king of the vampires. And vampires don't chat. So I didn't write him any dialogue.

Chris Lee has claimed that he refused to speak the lines he was given. On the other hand, there's a story that Chris called Peter Cushing and told him he was about to do this movie, written by Jimmy Sangster, and he hadn't been given any lines to say. Peter told him to be thankful for small mercies.

So you can take your pick as to why Christopher Lee didn't have any dialogue in the picture. Or you can take my word for it. I didn't write any.

As one of the critics said, 'Christopher Lee, blood-shot and speechless, makes a powerful figure out of

CLASSIC SCENE

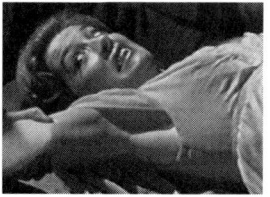

DRACULA PRINCE OF DARKNESS

*T*here are two scenes I already mentioned which stand out for me. The resurrection of Dracula with the body of Alan suspended above the coffin, and the subsequent materialising of Dracula, particularly well done given the paucity of the special effects budget. The other is the staking of Helen.

Another scene I particularly liked was the 'suck the blood from my chest' scene between Dracula and the prim and proper Diana.

These were the three scenes that gave us most trouble with the censor. The first two because they were too bloody, the third was considered too erotic. We fought long and hard over these scenes, but we fought long and hard with the censor a lot of the time. And exactly the same resurrection scene was used later in Lust for a Vampire (which I didn't write) and, to the best of my knowledge, caused no problems whatsoever.

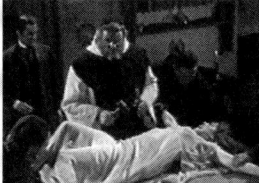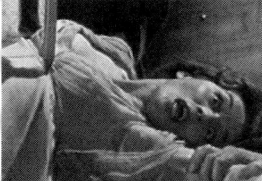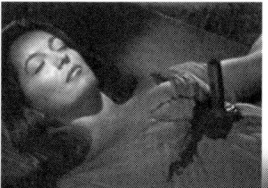

Dracula' (*Kine Weekly*), while the *Times* reckoned, 'The latest Dracula is the best they've made up to now.'

I don't agree with the *Times*. At the risk of offending some of the aficionados I think the first *Dracula* was the best. It was all so new back then. Hammer weren't fully aware of what they'd got hold of, so they weren't trying to repeat the formula. They were creating the formula, and by the time *Prince of Darkness* came out it was getting well-worn.

Nevertheless, there were some very good sequences in this movie. Worth pointing out perhaps is the fact that nothing actually happens until we're nearly 40 minutes in, when Alan is stabbed by Klove. Up to that point we've had mystery and tension combined with expectation, but that's it. It's a confirmation of my theory of suspense. You can keep the audience dangling for a long, long time providing

they know something pretty terrible is eventually going to take place. Then once the action starts it really gets going. The bloodletting scene is particularly well shot. I said earlier that there were censor problems with this sequence. Even now I don't know how we got away with it. Same with the sequence where the Barbara Shelley character is staked through the heart in the monastery. Previous stakings had always been performed on what was virtually a corpse. But this scene, with Shelley yelling and screaming, struggling to free herself from the grip of two or three monks, was in my opinion pretty powerful.

The only thing I miss is the lack of a 'pass the marmalade' scene. I don't have a copy of my script so I don't even know if I wrote one. It's hard to believe I didn't. On the other hand, this is a pretty grim bunch of people, maybe there just wasn't room for a laugh.

CHAPTER 15

The Anniversary

THE ANNIVERSARY

(filmed 1 May to 10 May 1967,
filming remounted 15 May to 12 July 1967,
released 11 January 1968)

Tony Hinds asked me to go to the theatre to see a play called *The Anniversary* written by Bill MacIlwraith. It was a good play with a wonderfully over-the-top central character played by Mona Washbourne. As I recall, Tony even paid for my seats. I should have known there was something afoot.

Next day. Lunch. Did I think it would be a good part for Bette Davis? I told him I thought it would be a wonderful part for Bette Davis. Would I like to write the movie? Seeing my last picture had been a Bulldog Drummond subject for Rank which the *Motion Picture Guide* had called 'overlong and silly', I decided a change of scene might be a good idea. So, in spite of slight doubts about whether the play would actually transfer to the screen, I accepted the deal, borrowed a copy of the play and wrote the first draft, handing it in around four weeks later.

In retrospect, I feel my doubts were justified. The piece did not lend itself to being turned into a movie. Some plays do, in spite of their confinement. Unfortunately *The Anniversary* wasn't one of them. I think the powers that be felt that, providing they could get Bette Davis again, then to hell with what she was in, just so long as she was up there on the screen.

The making of *The Anniversary* turned out to be one of those not infrequent occasions when the drama off stage is more tangled, more aggravating, more emotionally charged, than what gets up there on screen. Basically the story is about the domineering Mrs Taggart, who has summoned her three sons to her home to celebrate her wedding anniversary to a husband who is long dead. Slowly, during the course of the evening she manages to destroy all of their plans for the future, which mainly involve getting away from her sphere of influence. Having successfully destroyed them all and sent them on their way, she raises her glass to a portrait of her dead husband. 'It's been a lovely day, dad. Till next year!'

Tony suggested a few changes in the script and, *en passant*, he asked if I would like to produce it.

'No way,' says I.

'Please,' says Tony.

'Not for all the money in the world,' says I.

'How much money is that?' asked Tony.

I told him, he agreed, and Monica packed her bags and went to our house in the South of France as she had threatened, leaving the country the same day Bette arrived.

But before that we had to go through the whole 'auditioning the director' bit again. I had tried to get Seth Holt, who would have been ideal for the movie, but he was off in cloud cuckoo land making a movie with Zero Mostel. As I said, two fat crazies together. Word was that when the money people saw what was happening on screen, they pulled the plug. Unfortunately they didn't pull it soon enough for me and we had to find somebody else. Daniel Petrie, who had directed *The Stolen Hours*, a remake of the 1939 Bette Davis movie *Dark Victory* (for which she had been

The monstrous Mrs Taggart (Bette Davis) in **The Anniversary** *(1968).*

nominated for an Oscar), was considered as a second choice. There was a disagreement, and Petrie was out. Next up, Alvin Rakoff.

Alvin was a very good TV director, part of the group who worked for Sidney Newman who created *Armchair Theatre*. He came highly recommended. Phone calls were made and Bette Davis said that he sounded okay but she'd have to meet him first before making her final decision. So Alvin and I duly got ourselves onto an aeroplane to Los Angeles. Bette had moved from Stone Canyon and was now living in an apartment off Wilshire Boulevard in Beverly Hills, right behind the Regent Beverly Wilshire hotel, famous then because Warren Beatty lived there and now because that's where they shot *Pretty Woman*.

We met her for dinner the night we arrived and the following day Bette and I had a meeting. She asked a few questions and finally said she was happy to go ahead with Alvin. She'd have preferred Seth, but *c'est la vie*. I didn't feel 100 per cent happy about her attitude, which I indicated in a telephone message back to Hammer in London. 'Miss Davis has approved Alvin Rakoff... Not altogether plain sailing.' Forecast of bad times ahead.

I wanted to get straight back onto an aeroplane home but she insisted that I stay and have dinner with her that night. She was living with her daughter BD at the time and she wanted to give us both a home-cooked meal. But this was purely social so I wasn't to bring Alvin, which suited him down to the ground because he had a whole bunch of friends he wanted to hang out with. I should have known I was in for trouble because as I arrived the chauffeur was just taking BD off to the movies. Bette and I were to have a dinner à *deux*.

And a very nice dinner it was too. She was a very good cook. It wasn't until coffee time that she started chasing me around the sofa. I mean actually chasing me around the sofa like some dreadful scene from an old Chaplin movie. In the end I had to pretend to be a lot drunker than I was and pass out. I knew that if I could keep my trousers on until 10.30 pm BD would be home and my virtue would remain intact. This I did and I have great respect for Bette in that she never held it against me. I think she hoped I'd forgotten the whole incident. The following night I hung out with Alvin and had a great time, before climbing on an aeroplane once more.

Back in England, we finished the pre-production work which included the construction of a set representing the house where Mrs Taggart lived. It was a huge set on three levels, beautifully designed by art director Reece Pemberton. One of its features was a wide staircase leading straight down to the main living room. At the top of the staircase was a landing with a couple of bedrooms leading off and another set of stairs leading up to the third level. I only mention all this because of what happened later.

We cast Jack Hedley, Sheila Hancock and James Cossins, all of whom had been in the play, together with Elaine Taylor and Christian Roberts. A good, solid cast who, in spite of all the aggro that followed, turned in first-rate performances. Finally, Bette Davis arrived and immediately the atmosphere became tense. I wrote at the beginning of this book that I was sure some of the bad memories would come creeping back once I got into my stride, that 'Somewhere back there during the last 50 years there must have been a couple of bad days. But for the life of me, I can't recall them right now.' Okay! Cancel that. I recall them in all their gory detail.

First up, Bette arrives, her 'entourage' consisting this time of just one middle-aged, gently gay ex-hairdresser. And at their first meeting she tells Sheila Hancock that she would have infinitely preferred Jill Bennett in the part – not a statement designed to win friends and influence people.

But the main problem on *The Anniversary* had nothing to do with Sheila Hancock. It was with Alvin Rakoff. Two days into shooting and we were a day behind schedule and slipping fast. By the end of the first week we were three days behind and all was doom and gloom. Bette hated everyone and everyone hated her. Most of all she hated Alvin.

After five days she summoned me to her dressing room one evening after shooting. I knew what her opening line would be before she opened her mouth. 'I've starred in 63 movies... [she'd obviously started including *The Nanny* in her CV] ...and this is the first time I've ever had to work for the camera. The camera *always* works for me.' She went on to say that 'Rakoff

Sheila Hancock and Christian Roberts in **The Anniversary** *(1968). Note the repositioned staircase.*

doesn't have the first fundamental knowledge of making a motion picture, let alone what an actor is all about.'

What she was getting at was Alvin's *modus operandi*. He was a TV director, accustomed to blocking out the actor's movements on the set before running the scene, something that was absolutely essential in those days because they were still putting out live drama. He'd worked very hard doing his homework and knew in his head exactly how he wanted the scene to play. Bette Davis enters on this line, crosses the room as she speaks that line, hits

*James Cossins, Jimmy, Bette Davis and director Roy Ward Baker lead the crew of **The Anniversary** in celebrating Independence Day on 4 July 1967.*

those marks we've put down there where she lights a cigarette, then she crosses the room to those other marks where she stubs it out as she says so and so. For television in those days, this was how they worked. But not in movies. Bette's argument was 'Maybe I don't want to light my cigarette there. How do I know until we've played the scene a couple of times?'

Then she'd quote her William Wyler story. 'Mr Wyler would call all the actors onto the set and say "This is the scene, play it." We'd play it while he watched. He'd make a couple of suggestions and we'd play it again. A couple more suggestions, then a couple more. Finally, when we were playing the

scene we all felt comfortable with, he would turn to his cinematographer and say "That's the scene, photograph it."'

How true this was I never knew, but it sounded very reasonable to me. 'I'll tell Alvin,' I said, wondering how the hell I was going to do that. But I didn't have to worry. Bette Davis hadn't finished. 'I can't work with him any more,' she said. 'He'll have to go.'

I called Tony Hinds at head office. He was the executive producer on this one. At least he didn't jump into his car and drive off. We got onto the money people in Los Angeles. 'Bette Davis wants to fire the director.'

So what's your problem, they wanted to know. Then, just so we'd be sure where we stood, they went on to say that *The Anniversary* wasn't an Alvin Rakoff film, neither was it an Anthony Hinds or Jimmy Sangster film. And, if push came to shove, it wasn't even a Hammer film. It was a Bette Davis film. End of discussion.

Poor Alvin, who I'm sure had no idea the shit was going to hit the fan at all, let alone with such force, packed his briefcase and quietly left. I'm sure this did his career no good at all, and to this day I feel sorry for what happened. But the show must go on. We had to find another director and we had to do it fast. Bette Davis asked me to take over. Fortunately I had the good sense to say no.

Roy Ward Baker had just finished directing *Quatermass and the Pit* for Hammer and was an old friend of Bette's from his Hollywood days. Yes, he was prepared to take over and yes, Bette Davis was willing for him to do so. Saved by the gong, I thought. But Roy is nobody's fool. He knew we'd already shot a week and he didn't want any of Alvin's material going into the final cut. Who knows, there could have been a credit dispute. So he told us he didn't like the way the staircase came down into the centre of the main room, he'd prefer it to come down at an angle. Result, we had to rebuild the set and everything shot to date had to be thrown out.

So there we were, week three into the schedule, and not a foot of film in the can. When I first started with Hammer back in 1949, by week three we'd practically finished the movie.

It would be nice to be able to say that from then on everything was sweetness and light. It wasn't. The other members of the cast had been very fond of Alvin and they took his leaving very badly. They were all professional enough not to let it show in their performances, but the atmosphere on the set was wicked. Added to this, with the exception of cinematographer Harry Waxman, who was worried about the Six Day War in Israel, the camera crew was made up of untalented prima donnas. The focus puller quit because he said Roy Baker was rude to him and the operator, who'd nearly quit when he heard Roy was taking over the movie, never stopped telling me 'I told you so,' referring to his warning to me that there'd be

Pervert Henry Taggart (James Cossins) is caught in the act by Shirley Blair (Elaine Taylor) in **The Anniversary** *(1968).*

trouble with Roy. The only trouble with Roy was he did the job as best he could but managed to get up everybody's nose in the process.

But all things come to an end. Bette Davis left. My wife returned from France. We put the picture together and, unfortunately, it wasn't nearly as good as it could have been. We really *needed* Seth Holt on that movie. As Bette had said, he was a 'mountain of evil' and would have made a great job of bringing Mrs Taggart to life.

The reviews were mixed. 'A frequently funny black comedy' (the *Sun*). 'Unnerving, yet wickedly funny' (*Sunday Express*). The Americans weren't so sure. The *New York Post* said it was 'so exaggerated that it shatters the credibility needed to be effective satire,' while *Variety*, the showbusiness bible, said it was 'a vehicle for the extravagant tantrums of Bette Davis.'

I should give the last word to Alvin Rakoff. He was quoted as calling it 'a mess of a film built around Davis' foolish, overbaked posturings and camera hoggings.'

Well he would, wouldn't he? But he was dead right.

CHAPTER 16

Crescendo

CRESCENDO

(studio filming 14 July to 23 August 1969, released 7 May 1970)

Crescendo was the last of the psycho-type movies I wrote for Hammer. I'm not counting *Fear in the Night* because, that one, I produced and directed. A different kettle of fish entirely, as you will read later.

For a long time I claimed a co-screenplay credit with Alfred Shaughnessy, a man I didn't even meet until 20 years later. I have also been quoted as saying I didn't know whether he rewrote me or I rewrote him. I saw the movie recently and I obviously rewrote him because the screenplay credit reads 'Screenplay by Jimmy Sangster and Alfred Shaughnessy. Based on an original screenplay by Alfred Shaughnessy'. So there we have it. I mentioned it to Freddy Shaugnessy last time I saw him, and he hadn't remembered the sequence of events either. He did say in his autobiography, *A Confession in Writing*, that he wrote it against his better judgment... 'when money was short and I had to accept whatever was on offer to pay the rent. Some writers call this 'whoring'.'

I was a writer too. I always called it making a living. But then I was only writing horror-type movies, while Freddy wrote such blockbusters as *Follow That Horse* and *Room in the House*.

Apparently he wrote it with the idea of Michael Reeves directing. He called it *Apassionata*. A cast was lined up – Christopher Lee, Flora Robson and Susan Hampshire – and the movie was about to go with distributors Compton Films when it all fell through.

Deals had a habit of doing that in those days too. Mike Reeves was a very clever young director (best known for *Witchfinder General*) who unfortunately was found dead in his apartment in London, having overdosed on booze and drugs. At 25 years old, a great waste of a large talent.

Anyway, the script that Freddy 'whored' did various rounds, being rewritten by John Gilling with talk of Joan Crawford doing the movie, eventually landing on Hammer's doorstep. And Hammer, as was their wont in those days, gave it to me to do some rewrites. I have to admit to not liking the story much when I first read it, and not liking it much more when I'd done the rewrites.

It was set in the South of France, close to the Camargue, where we had shot *Maniac*. I think Michael Carreras had become enamoured with the area. But that was only the setting. I have a copy of the script, with some of Michael's notes scribbled in it. One is re the Camargue.

The 2nd unit location is budgeted at £2500. We will use the Le Touquet area...

Then, after the first script heading (EXT. CAMARGUE. DAY.), Michael has written

Stock footage plus 2nd unit and studio front projection.

These notes point to the fact that they didn't go to the

Susan Roberts (Stefanie Powers) prepares a dose of painkilling heroin in **Crescendo** *(1970).*

Camargue at all and I have to admit to not knowing why they bothered faking it in the first place. Okay, so the Camargue was a very dramatic area, but the story could have been located anywhere and certainly didn't gain anything from the location.

The plot involves an attractive young music teacher, Susan Roberts (Stefanie Powers), who comes to France to research a biography on the life of the late Henry Ryman, a celebrated American classical composer. She has been invited by Ryman's widow, Danielle (Margaretta Scott), to stay at the family château. There she is introduced to Danielle's wheelchair-bound son, Georges (James Olson), who is addicted to heroin as a pain killer. The stuff is administered by Liliane (Jane Lapotaire), the not very sexy French maid, who, as well as shooting him up, also strips in front of him and seduces him, aiming eventually to marry him. Susan comes across a photograph of a woman who looks a bit like she does and Danielle tells her that her name was

Georges Ryman (James Olson) and his equally deranged mother Danielle (Margaretta Scott) in **Crescendo** *(1970).*

Catherine and she was the woman her son was in love with, but after his accident she left him.

Mysterious happenings start to take place, as they usually do in this kind of a movie. Piano playing in the middle of the night for instance, the whole thing culminating in the stabbing of Liliane in the pool by an unseen assassin. The following morning the pool has been emptied and cleaned. Then Georges suffers another painful attack and this time it is Susan who gives him his heroin. Danielle later tells her that, in France, not only is the drug addict subject to imprisonment but so is the administrator of the drug. But she won't say a word if Susan stays around and eventually marries Georges.

During all this, Georges is haunted by a nightmare where he is making love to a woman and is shot by an unidentified stranger. Eventually Susan discovers that Georges has a mad twin brother, Jacques (also James Olson), who was married to Catherine and who killed her when she discovered she was having an affair with his brother Georges. Now he thinks Susan is Catherine. He stalks her and is about to rape/kill her, when Danielle appears and shoots him in the back. Susan flees the château, leaving behind Georges and Danielle, who had hatched an insane plot to carry on the Ryman music legacy through the birth of Jacques' child with Susan.

Reading that back, one wonders how some of these films ever got off the drawing board. Before an original script is written there are various stages it has to go through. First you have to sell the idea; a couple of lines should do it. Next up: the storyline, which is what you've just read. Then, if you're lucky, a treatment, followed by, if you're even luckier, a screenplay. So, with a story like the above, how did this piece ever get off the ground? It got off the ground because the writer went straight to screenplay.

Take a sequence that, in a storyline, reads: 'Awakened by piano music in the middle of the night, Susan heads for the poolhouse from where it's coming.' Now read it in the screenplay...

EXT. CHATEAU. NIGHT.
Susan, dressed in her flimsy nightdress, comes out of the main house and looks towards the poolhouse from where the piano playing that

awakened her is coming. This is the place where the dead Henry Ryman worked until he died. The place that nobody in the house ever uses. A place of darkness and mystery. There is a light burning from inside. Slowly, slowly, she starts towards the poolhouse as the sound of the music swells. Around her the night, with its unknown mysteries and horrors, crowds in. Closer, closer... unable to take her eyes off the terror that she somehow knows she is going to find.

Same stage directions but dressed up a little to convey the scene rather than just the situation. In other words, a selling document. But, as a writer, you've got to be prepared to invest a good deal of time and effort into writing a spec screenplay, with every chance it will never see the light of day. I've got two in my bottom drawer right now, both comedies. Maybe I should have stuck to doing what I obviously did best, namely horror films. But I did manage to sell a 15-year-old screenplay to German TV a couple of years back. In the case of *Crescendo*, Alfred Shaughnessy came up with the story idea, went to screenplay and sold it. He invested the time and effort, and eventually it paid off. The fact that somebody (me) messed with it later is par for the course, something I've written about elsewhere. But I digress.

The film was the first Hammer psycho thriller since *The Nanny* four years earlier. There'd been a bunch of 'prehistorics', a couple of Draculas, a couple of Frankensteins but no 'things that go bump in the dark'. So why did they decide to go with *Crescendo*? There was no big American star attached. James Olson was a minor actor and he gave a minor, rather over-the-top performance. He'd just finished starring in Hammer's *Moon Zero Two*. Maybe they decided to save money on the air fare. He's here so put him in the picture. I'm not saying he was bad, it's just that he wasn't very good. But then I don't think anybody could have been really *good* in that part. The material just wasn't there.

Stefanie Powers was pretty and adequate, playing a very similar part to the one she had played in *Fanatic* five years earlier. For the director, Alan Gibson, this was his first feature film. A former television director, he didn't really show much flair for the genre. He went on to shoot a couple of modern day Dracula films for

Jane Lapotaire as French maid Liliane in **Crescendo** *(1970).*

Hammer, *Dracula A.D. 1972* and *The Satanic Rites oif Dracula*, which impressed neither critics nor box office.

The main set, designed by Scott MacGregor, built at ABPC Elstree, was extremely good, if a little lifeless. In fact, although I worked for Hammer three more times, the word 'lifeless' had begun to describe the whole Hammer scene. Tony Hinds had lost interest. Michael Carreras wanted to test pastures new. There was just Sir James and, as long as he was the boss, he continued to flog a dying horse for the next couple of years, culminating in 1973, when he finally sold the company.

As for the cause of the decline, I can only hazard a guess. By 1973 I was permanently based in Los Angeles, so I was no longer involved with Hammer on anything but a freelance basis. Okay, so I was involved in three later movies for Hammer, which, if you're still with me, you'll read about next. But I was away from the centre of things. I think Sir James was chasing a market that no longer existed or, if it did, didn't need the Hammer label attached to the product. Sex and nudity were what was demanded and there were any number of people who served it up better than Hammer was able. In short, I think this period marked the beginning of the end for Hammer.

CHAPTER 17

The Horror of Frankenstein

THE HORROR OF FRANKENSTEIN

(filmed 16 March to 29 April 1970,
released 8 October 1970)

The Horror of Frankenstein came to me out of left field. I was living in Los Angeles, just having done a *Movie of the Week* script for a producer named Aaron Spelling. *Taste of Evil* I called it, which was pretty dumb of me because it was a direct crib from *Taste of Fear* which I'd made ten years earlier and assumed was long forgotten by then. Unfortunately it had appeared on late-night TV a couple of weeks earlier and Aaron Spelling had seen it and noticed the similarity of the plot line. He mentioned the fact to my agent, who mentioned it to me.

'Aaron Spelling says there are similarities between the script you've just written for him and something he saw on the box last night.'

'At least I changed the names,' I said.

Anyway, Aaron went ahead and made the movie, with Barbara Stanwyck playing the Ann Todd part. I assume it worked for him because I did quite a few more jobs for him over the next few years.

I'd told my agent that I wanted to stay in Los Angeles and he was busy looking around for work when, out of the blue, I got this call from Hammer. Tony Hinds and Michael Carreras weren't around at the time, but Sir James decided it was time for yet another Frankenstein movie. They'd had a script written by a guy named Jeremy Burnham. He was an actor, having appeared in Hammer's *Brigand of Kandahar*. He'd also done some television writing. Hammer had obviously committed to the project, to be financed by ABPC, but

they told me the script needed some work done on it. Would I be interested in doing the rewrite? I told them I wasn't. What if they let me produce it? Still not interested. Been there, done that. Then I had an idea. I'd rewrite their script and produce it providing they let me direct as well. Short pause over the phone. They'd call me back. This they did about an hour later. Deal! The script's in the mail.

Three days later the script arrived. I read it and my heart sank. It was very similar to the script I'd written for Hammer umpteen years ago, the first Frankenstein movie they made. As far as I could see they needn't have bothered paying a writer to come up with something they as good as owned already. All of a sudden I didn't want to do it any more.

But a deal is a deal is a deal and I duly started to work on the script, trying to bring something different to it. I packed my bags, moved out of my apartment and went back to London where I eventually delivered my rewrites.

Since *my* last Frankenstein movie, *Revenge of...*, Hammer had made three more. In 1964 they released *The Evil of Frankenstein*. directed by Freddie Francis, produced by Tony Hinds and written by Tony under his pseudonym John Elder. This one bombed both with the critics and at the box office. But still they pushed on. *Frankenstein Created Woman* was their next effort. Terry Fisher returned to the fold to direct this one. Anthony Nelson Keys produced it and John Elder once more wrote the screenplay. This one was received much better. So much so that they went for a third,

Ralph Bates as Hammer's new Baron in **The Horror of Frankenstein** *(1970).*

RALPH BATES

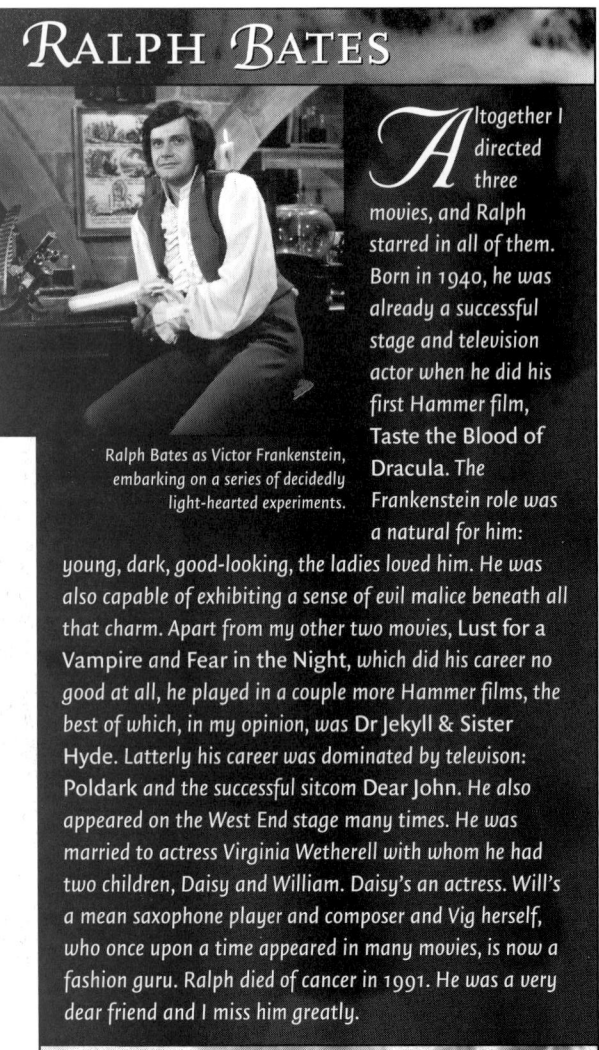

Ralph Bates as Victor Frankenstein, embarking on a series of decidedly light-hearted experiments.

Altogether I directed three movies, and Ralph starred in all of them. Born in 1940, he was already a successful stage and television actor when he did his first Hammer film, **Taste the Blood of Dracula**. The Frankenstein role was a natural for him: young, dark, good-looking, the ladies loved him. He was also capable of exhibiting a sense of evil malice beneath all that charm. Apart from my other two movies, **Lust for a Vampire** and **Fear in the Night**, which did his career no good at all, he played in a couple more Hammer films, the best of which, in my opinion, was **Dr Jekyll & Sister Hyde**. Latterly his career was dominated by television: Poldark and the successful sitcom Dear John. He also appeared on the West End stage many times. He was married to actress Virginia Wetherell with whom he had two children, Daisy and William. Daisy's an actress. Will's a mean saxophone player and composer and Vig herself, who once upon a time appeared in many movies, is now a fashion guru. Ralph died of cancer in 1991. He was a very dear friend and I miss him greatly.

Frankenstein Must Be Destroyed. Again Terry directed, but this time the script was written by Tony Keys, who also produced, and the assistant director, Bert Batt. Fair enough, that's how I started. Apparently this one was *very* well received. So let's do it again, they decided, and let's ask Sangster to do it.

As in the Jeremy Burnham script, the story was very much as before. This wasn't a *Return of...* or a *Revenge of...* This was back to square one, opening with the young Victor (Ralph Bates) at school where he outshines the teacher and, in my version, seduces most of his female fellow students. Then, the Burnham script took a quick cut to a few years later, finding Victor at university receiving news of his father's death. I stayed within the current time frame for a few more scenes where, back at the castle, Victor's father (George Belbin) is having it off with the housekeeper, Alys (Kate O'Mara). Tired of waiting for his inheritance, and eager to get out from under the control of his father, Victor fixes the old boy's shotgun so that it blows his head off while he's out shooting. And off he goes to the University of Vienna.

There he starts his experiments with the help of a fellow student, Wilhelm (Graham James). Six years later, after Victor has got the Dean's daughter pregnant, he and Wilhelm return to Castle Frankenstein to continue in their search for the secret of life. There we meet all his old school chums, Elizabeth (Veronica Carlson), Henry Becker (Jon Finch), who is now Chief of Police, and, last but not least, the housekeeper, Alys, with whom he takes over where his father left off. After various experiments, Victor starts to put together a man, to the disgust of Wilhelm, hiring a graverobber (Dennis Price) to supply him with corpses. Wilhelm eventually threatens to go to the authorities, so Victor kills him, using his hands for his new creation. He poisons Elizabeth's father (Bernard Archard) and removes his brain. Then the graverobber drops it and Victor throws him into the acid tank.

Eventually the monster (David Prowse) is activated and Victor uses him to kill both Alys and then the graverobber's wife (Joan Rice), both of whom were becoming suspicious. Then, after escaping, the monster returns to the castle and confronts Elizabeth. She is saved by Victor, who hides the monser in an empty tank while he placates the police and the local villagers. Unfortunately, a little village girl tugs on a rope, releasing acid into the tank, completely destroying the monster, and leaving Victor very aggrieved.

The Burnham script was quite different from all this and, in my opinion, was too similar (and not as good as) the first couple of *Frankenstein* movies. I wanted to do something really different, so I stuck my tongue firmly in my cheek and I pressed on. Like I said, it was the basic mixture very much as before but, I hoped, with a couple of laughs thrown in. After all, who wanted to make the same picture twice? I

CLASSIC SCENE

 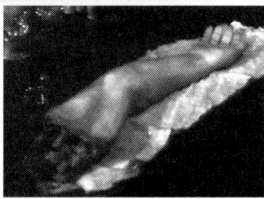  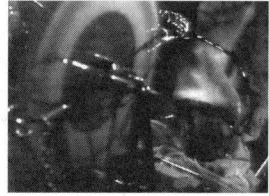

THE HORROR OF FRANKENSTEIN

𝓜y favourite scene, although you can hardly call it 'classic', is the scene where Victor demonstrates to Wilhelm the severed arm he has rigged up as part of his experiments at university. He tells Wilhelm he's going to send it to the Dean, whose daughter he's just made pregnant. Then, switching on the electric source it's connected to, we watch it lift up and give the V-sign. I had to shoot two versions of this. The Americans only use one finger to deliver the same message.

 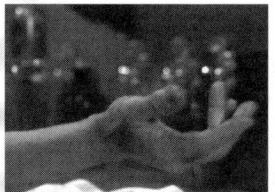  

delivered the script to Hammer and it was pronounced acceptable. In fact, I honestly don't think anybody read it. Tony Hinds had quit Hammer, content in the future to just write for them, and Michael Carreras was off doing his own thing. The company was being run by Sir James, with the help of his long-time assistant Brian Lawrence, who had been with the company since day one. Neither of them knew anything about production. As far as they were concerned, Sangster was making a *Frankenstein* movie. He knows what he's doing so let him get on with it.

I had an apartment in the Carlton Tower Hotel at that time which I used as an office. It was there that I did my casting. Everything went fine except for the two major parts, Baron Frankenstein and the Monster. There was no question of using Peter Cushing again because I'd written the part much younger. Sir James wanted me to cast the actor they'd just used in *Taste the Blood of Dracula*, Ralph Bates. I didn't think he was right and told him so. 'At least meet the man,' said Sir James, who was grooming Ralph to take over the Peter

Cushing parts in any number of upcoming movies. Not, I hasten to say, because they wanted to break with Peter. It was just that he was getting a little old to carry off the sex symbol image that Hammer was into selling by now. So I duly met Ralph, was suitably impressed and he got the part. A couple of days later I cast David Prowse as the monster and we were off and running.

I have to admit here that I have never had such an enjoyable time as I did during the six weeks we were shooting *The Horror of Frankenstein*. I loved every minute of it. Ralph Bates became a very good friend and later asked me to be godfather to his son William. The crew were wonderful. Scott MacGregor skimped a bit on the sets, but the cameraman Moray Grant did a first-class job and his operator Neil Binney saved my bacon more times than I can remember. I'd line up a shot, rehearse it, then very quietly ask Neil whether it would cut with the last shot. He'd give me a yea or nay. Another great help was Betty Harley, the continuity girl. At the end of a sequence I'd ask her if I'd covered everything I

*David Prowse as the Monster in **The Horror of Frankenstein** (1970).*

needed. Mostly she'd say yes. Occasionally she'd tell me maybe an extra close-up there wouldn't come amiss. Don't forget, this was my first time out behind the camera. I needed all the help I could get.

We kept to schedule and budget and we never stopped laughing. I read somewhere that Veronica Carlson, whom both Ralph and I lusted after (in an entirely innocent manner as far as I was concerned), said that Ralph and I didn't take the shooting seriously and had a jolly good laugh. Certainly we had a good laugh, but we also took the making of the picture very seriously. At least I did. And I'm pretty sure Ralph did too. Because we were enjoying ourselves it didn't mean we were turning out bad work.

Some people say that is one of the reasons why it wasn't a very good movie. On the other hand, I viewed it recently and I think it garnered far more stick than it deserved. I meant it to be lighthearted. Unfortunately it was so lighthearted its feet never touched the ground. Problem was, the long-serving Hammer fans felt let down and the new, younger audience didn't go for it either.

I think one of the reasons it wasn't as good a movie as it should have been was that there was nobody to keep me in check. I was the writer/producer/director, the closest you can get to being God. Nobody was around to say 'You can't do this' or 'That doesn't work.' James Carreras never saw the rushes and never visited the studio.

I can think of any number of changes that would or would not have taken place had a Michael Carreras or a Tony Hinds been sitting up there in Hammer House. For example, there is a scene where Victor and Wilhelm, out riding, interrupt a hold-up of a coach by highwaymen. I did any number of location shots of the two guys riding, spotting the hold-up and heading down to the rescue. Then, for reasons I can't even begin to guess at from this distance, instead of finishing the sequence on location, I decided to take over the largest stage at Elstree and have it dressed as a forest clearing, so I could shoot the balance of the sequence indoors.

I was always happier shooting in the studio. There you had absolute control. It didn't matter what the weather was or how much extraneous noise there was and there were no spectators crowding around, getting in the way. But, in this particular case, apart from the expense, it didn't look nearly as good as it would have had I shot it on location. Tony or Michael, quite rightly, wouldn't have allowed me to get away with it. But with Jimmy Sangster as producer, Jimmy Sangster the director could get away with whatever he wanted, and vice versa. As for Jimmy Sangster the writer, usually nobody takes any notice of the writer on the set, most times they won't even let him in the

*Jimmy and **Horror of Frankenstein** leading lady Veronica Carlson at Elstree Studios in spring 1970.*

CLASSIC SCENE

THE HORROR OF FRANKENSTEIN

For all the wrong reasons, my second favourite scene is the one where Victor carries the unconscious Elizabeth from the laboratory, where she's just been attacked by the Monster, back to her bedroom. I love this scene because of the problem Ralph had in carrying Veronica. She was too heavy for him. If you look closely, you can see the effort on his face. If we hadn't got it in the first take... forget it.

 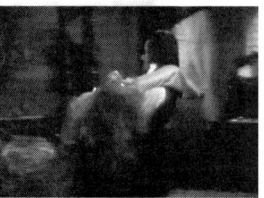  

studio. On this occasion, the writer came into his own. If I wanted a change in the script I'd ask the director, he'd ask the producer, and they'd tell me, the writer, 'Okay.'

In spite of that, some of the critics seemed to like it. At least they understood what I was trying to get at: '....tongue in cheek horror', 'the first hour is not only painless but fun.' And from *Variety*, who really got the point: 'Lighthearted.'

And, in my opinion, that's exactly what it was. A lighthearted fairytale. Who could take seriously the opening sequence where he leads the girl off into the woods to help him with his 'scientific research' and her asking him if she should take her clothes off now. Then, later, some of the lines, like Wilhelm's 'Where do you inject a tortoise?' Or the gravedigger complaining about the shortage of bodies with the remark that 'Times are hard. People aren't dying off so quickly. It's the Welfare State.' Or my favourite, when the monster is finally animated and Victor gets over his surprise, sticking out his hand with a 'How do you do? I'm Victor Frankenstein.'

On the other hand ... other critics weren't so kind. 'A sorry mess indeed.' 'By all accounts it was fun to make, but that was where the fun ended.' 'It is difficult to defend the film on any level.'

Basically the movie failed both as a comedy and as a horror film. It wasn't funny enough for the first and it certainly wasn't horrific enough for the second. One of the problems, I feel, is that it was a 'Hammer Film', part of a cycle, promising the mixture as before. The fans didn't want 'tongue in cheek'. I'm not saying it would have been better to have been distributed as *Carry on Frankenstein* (which sounds like a fun idea), but I'm sure the fans felt cheated. When Mel Brooks made *Young Frankenstein* in 1974 everyone was perfectly happy because they were going to see a Mel Brooks film with all that that implied. When they went to see Hammer's *The Horror of Frankenstein*, thet didn't get what they paid for. Maybe I would have spotted all this in the cutting-room after we finished shooting, and maybe I could have done something about it. But we'll never know because three days after I finished shooting I went straight onto another movie.

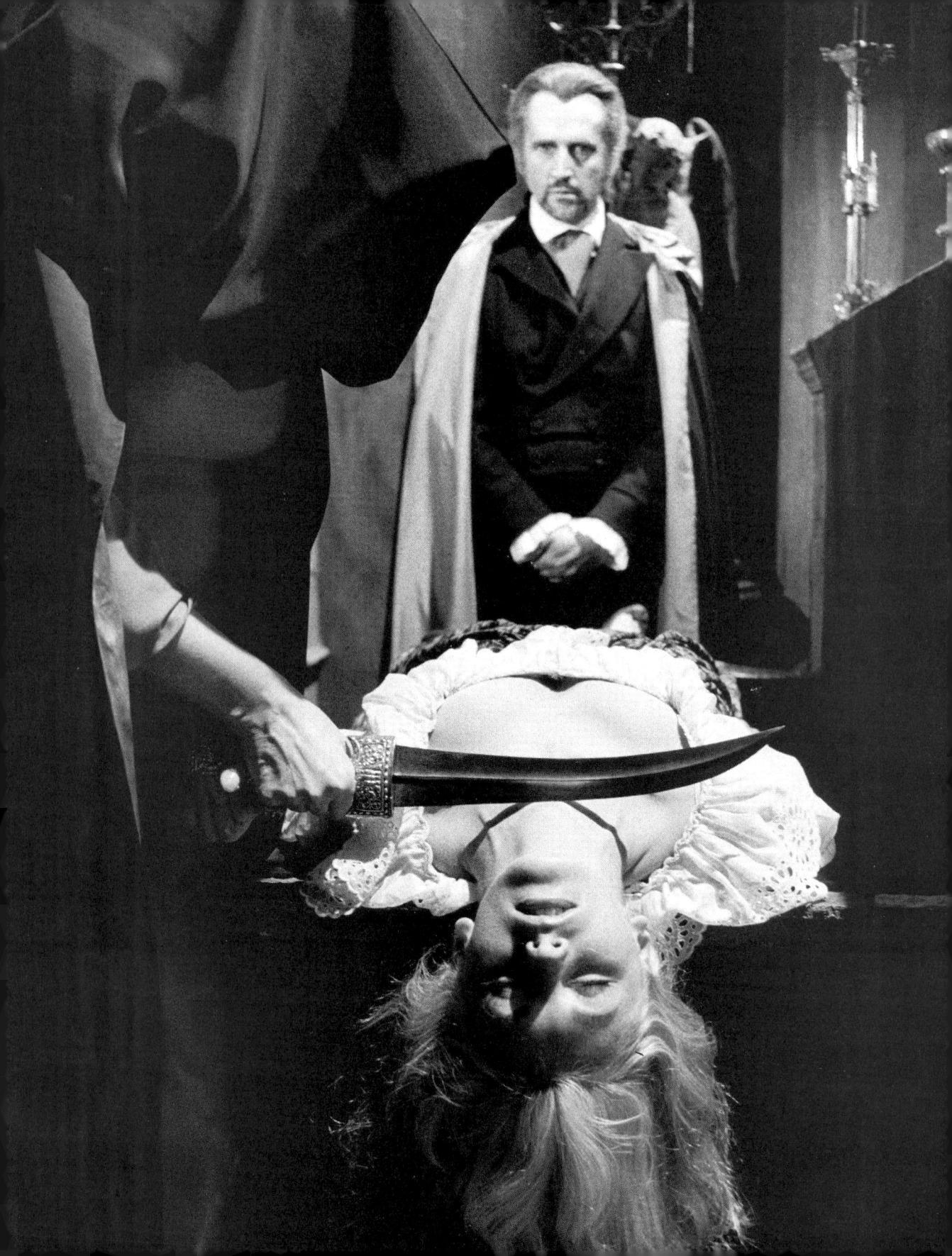

CHAPTER 18

*L*ust for a Vampire

LUST FOR A VAMPIRE
(filmed 6 July to 18 August 1970,
released 17 January 1971)

*L*ust for a Vampire. The title alone should have warned me off. In fact, when I came aboard it was called *To Love a Vampire*, which isn't quite as bad. Apparently the project was originally designed as a follow-up to *The Vampire Lovers*, produced by Harry Fine and Michael Style, which had been made in partnership with American International Pictures. But AIP backed out of this second Karnstein movie and it was temporarily shelved. It saw the light of day once more when ABPC agreed to finance it. This meant it had to be shot at ABPC's Elstree Studios.

Earlier on in this book, when I was writing about *X the Unknown*, I said that one of the worst things that can happen to a director is being hired when the movie has already been cast, the sets built and they've dotted the i's and crossed the t's in the script. This was the case here.

The script, by Tudor Gates, was okay. There were a couple of things I would have done to it if I'd had the time. Probably more than a couple. But I didn't have the time and the producers didn't want me messing with it anyway.

The story was very much the mixture as before. It was round about here that Hammer started to feel that they might be flogging a dead horse, even though they went on doing it for the next two or three years. It opened in the usual sparklingly clean village somewhere in middle Europe where every 40 years the

Karnstein family return to terrorise the villagers and surrounding countryside. A village girl is kidnapped and dragged off to the castle where she has her throat cut. The blood is used to resurrect the long-dead Carmilla, henceforth to be known as Mircalla.

Enter our hero Richard LeStrange (Michael Johnson), an author researching a book. He visits the castle and is scared by a group of cowled figures who turn out to be young girls from the local finishing school, escorted by their history master Giles Barton (Ralph Bates). Richard cons his way onto the staff of the school when he spots Mircalla, who has just been enrolled by her aunt, Countess Herritzen (Barbara Jefford), who is really Countess Karnstein. Mircalla befriends an American pupil, Susan (Pippa Steel), and eventually chews on her neck and kills her. Barton finds the body and, realising the true identity of

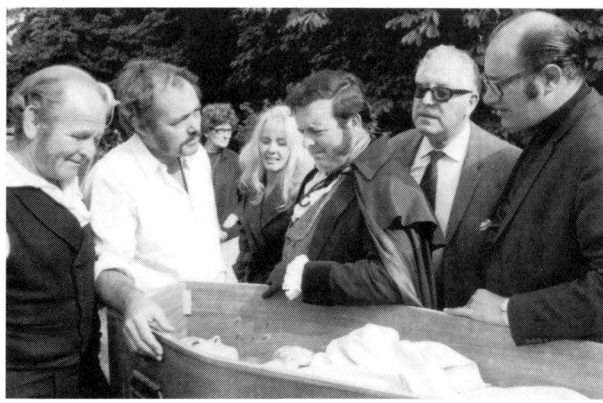

Left: Count Karnstein (Mike Raven) presides over the ritual sacrifice of a peasant girl (Kirsten Lindholm) in **Lust for a Vampire**, released in 1971.
Above: Chris Cunningham, Jimmy, Yutte Stensgaard, David Healy, producers Harry Fine and Michael Style and Pippa Steel (in coffin) pictured during the location shooting of **Lust for a Vampire** in summer 1970.

Mircalla, he dumps Susan in a well and then tells Mircalla that he knows about her and begs to be able to serve her. She kills him too.

Richard now tells her he's in love with her and she succumbs to his sexual advances. Janet, one of the teachers (Suzanna Leigh), who has fallen in love with Richard, calls the police to investigate the death of Susan. The police chief is murdered by Count Karnstein (Mike Raven). Mircalla later attempts to attack Janet but she is saved by the crucifix around her neck. Susan's father, Pelley (David Healy), arrives at the school and orders the body of the dead Susan to be exhumed. There, he sees the marks of the vampire on her neck. That night, Pelley and a conveniently visiting Bishop lead the villagers to the castle to burn it down. Inside, Count and Countess Karnstein and Mircalla wait. Fire will only destroy their bodies; their spirits will be free to enter new ones. But Richard intervenes to save Mircalla. The Count orders her to kill him. But, before she can reach him, a shaft of burning timber falls from the roof and effectively stakes her through the heart. Richard is dragged to safety by Pelley and embraced by Janet.

Terry Fisher had been hired to do the picture, but he took sick and really wasn't up to it. So, two weeks

Giles Barton (Ralph Bates) succumbs to Carmilla (Yutte Stensgaard) in **Lust for a Vampire***.*

before the scheduled start of shooting, Fine and Style, the producers, checked with James Carreras who gave them the go-ahead to hire me to take Terry's place. I was in the cutting rooms at Elstree at the time, editing *The Horror of Frankenstein*, when they came a-calling. 'Would I be interested?' Of course I was interested. I hadn't even finished my first movie as a director, and here they were clamouring at my door. God! How wrong can you be?

Peter Cushing had been cast in the part of Giles Barton, but his wife Helen became very ill just about then and he begged off. If Helen hadn't got sick, it would be interesting to know what excuse he would have come up with not to play the part, because he would have been a disaster in it, completely wrong from all directions. So the first thing Fine and Style asked me was who did I think should be cast to replace Peter. Out of desperation, I suggested Ralph Bates. At least that would mean I had a mate on the movie. They agreed with me. I think this was the last time they agreed with anything I suggested for the entire movie.

Ralph later said he agreed to do the movie 'as a favour to Jimmy. I thought it was a tasteless film and I regret having anything to do with it.'

Him and me both.

The rest of the cast were signed up already. Yutte Stensgaard, a pretty Danish actress/model, was playing Mircalla (an anagram of Carmilla; 'Alarmlic' would have been more appropriate). I read somewhere in an article by a man called Nicolas Barbano that the reason our Yutte wasn't a huge success in *Lust for a Vampire* was because it was a weak script, badly directed. I grant you, the script *was* weak and the direction wasn't all that it could have been. But Mr Barbano fails to mention that the main reason Yutte wasn't a success was because she wasn't a very good actress.

Then there was Mike Raven, an ex-Radio One disc jockey, playing Count Karnstein. He wasn't very good either. In fact they used Valentine Dyall to dub his voice after shooting and they used a shot of Christopher Lee's eyes from one of the Dracula movies for some of his close-ups.

The rest of the cast were okay. I understand Barbara Jefford, a superb actress, complained bitterly about her part, the movie, the director, the producers and the script. I sympathise with her, but she shouldn't

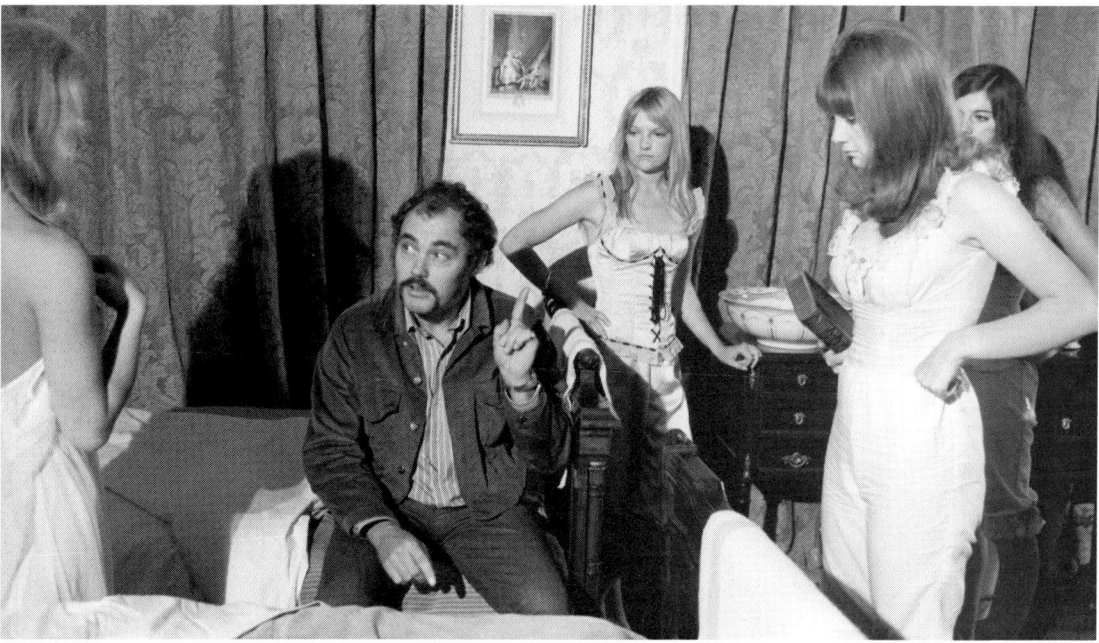

Directing the scenes in the girls' dormitory. A more explicit version was filmed for Continental audiences.

have signed on unless she needed the money very badly and, with Hammer footing the bill, there wouldn't even have been much of that. Then there were Suzanna Leigh and Michael Johnson, who were both very adequate, and finally David Healy, a wonderful American actor who was married to a charming Englishwoman who bred polo ponies.

Let me tell you about the producers, Harry Fine and Michael Style. They'd already shot *The Vampire Lovers*, also written by Tudor Gates. It had done pretty well at the box office. This was their follow-up. Roy Ward Baker had directed *The Vampire Lovers* for them. I never asked him how well he got on with Fine and Style. I also never asked why he didn't do this, their second movie for Hammer. Maybe he'd got lucky and was working on something else. As for me, I didn't get on with them at all.

Example. First day's shooting. Interior set at Elstree Studios. The coach drawn by four horses is driven into the schoolyard where it pulls up.

'Cut,' says I. 'Print it. Next set-up!'

'We can do better than that,' came a voice from the back. It was Michael Style, trying to behave the way he thought a producer should.

'You can do better than that? Then *you* shoot the fucking picture,' says I, heading for the nearest exit.

Slightly over-the-top reaction in retrospect, but I really meant it, especially as it was the first day of shooting and I had to establish my position with the crew. Michael Style went back to his office to sulk and I got on with the next shot. End of that particular incident. End also of any rapport between me and the producers. A producer is perfectly entitled to criticise the director. After all, he hired him and is responsible for paying his salary. But you don't do it in front of the entire crew on the first day of shooting. Also it helps if he knows what he's talking about, which Michael Style didn't. I don't think Harry Fine did either, but at least he stayed off the set.

I shot a sequence later of a bunch of sexy girls in diaphanous gowns dancing on the lawn outside the finishing school. The producers said I wasn't moving the camera enough. So I shot it again, moving the camera so much nobody knew where the hell they were. End result, we used the original version, which was what I intended.

I also shot a sequence which wasn't in the original script. At least, it *was* in the script but it finished well short of the scene I shot. This was the sex scene between Richard and Mircalla. The script read....

Richard moves in slowly to kiss her again, this time with great tenderness. Mircalla responds in the same way. Her lips brush his eyes... his cheeks... his throat as CAMERA MOVES INTO...

CLOSE RICHARD'S THROAT
Mircalla's lips part as though to give him a love bite.

CLOSE MIRCALLA
Her head jerks back suddenly as Richard (voice off) groans. Mircalla's eyes close. She gasps. Her teeth clench together. And then she pulls him closer to her and she weeps.

As far as the script was concerned, the scene ended there. As far as the finished movie was concerned, that's where the fun started. I went on to shoot a torrid, sexy scene. Two and a half minutes of it. This was one of those 'clear the set'-type sequences because the leading lady is going to take her clothes off. What actually happens in these cases, is visitors are banned but every electrician in the studio who's not actually working on a set climbs up onto our lighting gantry to cop a look. Happens all the time.

This was also the sequence that was covered musically by the dreadful song, 'Strange Love', that Harry Fine insisted on using. The story goes that he was so impressed by Harry Robinson's music for the picture that he went to James Carreras with the idea of using Robinson's love theme as a song which could be published as a boost for the movie. Phil Martell,

CLASSIC SCENE

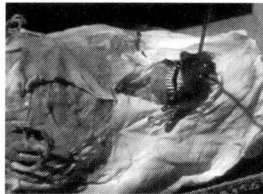

LUST FOR A VAMPIRE

I guess if one has to choose a 'classic' scene from the mish-mash that this movie turned out to be, it would have to be the revitalising of the Mircalla character when the Count pours fresh virgin's blood onto her shrouded figure. Yutte Stensgaard rising from the coffin is pretty good. The use of a close-up of Chris Lee's eyes from an entirely different film is not so good. I'd like to think the sexy love scene would be up there somewhere near the top of the list, but the song took care of that. So I feel the second scene worth mentioning is the sequence where the girl is dumped into the well (the filming of which is shown opposite). Good special effects here.

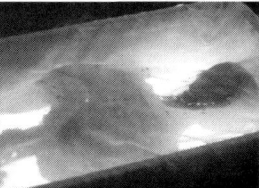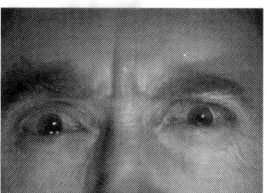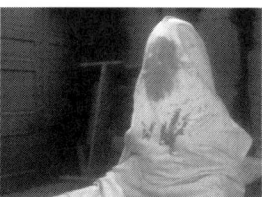

Hammer's musical director on more of their movies than I can remember, hated the idea and complained bitterly. But Harry Fine got his way and Frank Godwin, later to produce *Demons of the Mind* for Hammer, wrote the lyrics, which were sung by one 'Tracy'. Needless to say, I had no knowledge of this until at least six months later when I went to see the movie at the Odeon Hammersmith with Ralph Bates. I actually sank beneath my seat in embarrassment when it came up. In my opinion it really screwed up what could and should have been a very sexy scene.

But scenes like this couldn't save the movie. There was too much baggage aboard. The 'hero', as played by Michael Johnson, was a boozy lecher. The character, that is, not the actor, who was a charming, quite talented man. But, as Richard LeStrange, he was drunk as much as he was sober and he lusted after and seduced a girl of 17 or thereabouts. The fact that she was really around 150 didn't come into it, he *thought* she was 17. He fell in love with her after one scene, just

as the Suzanna Leigh character fell in love with him after two and a half minutes.

One small consolation. Unlike the old days when we made the first *Frankenstein* and *Dracula* movies, Hammer allowed me some peasants to storm the castle. Not a huge number of peasants, but when added to the Bishop's coach and the David Healy character riding a horse, quite an impressive mob. I've been told by people who've viewed the movie more times than is healthy that there's a shot of me somewhere during the procession, directing from another camera point. I've watched the bloody thing five times and I can't spot it.

Johnson and Del Vecchio got it right in their book when they said *Lust for a Vampire* is one of the few Hammer horrors to have nothing to recommend it. 'The film was a low point for the company and is embarrassing – or should be – for all concerned, including the audience.'

Forget the audience, guys. They couldn't have felt as embarrassed as I did.

CHAPTER 19

Fear in the Night

FEAR IN THE NIGHT
(filmed 15 November to 17 December 1971, released 9 July 1972)

Next came *Fear in the Night*. This was a script I had written almost ten years earlier earlier under the title *Brainstorm*. I'd written it for Hammer (and been paid) but then for various reasons they decided not to go ahead with it. It was taken out of the bottom drawer every now and then, the dust was blown off it and it was hawked around. They even changed the title to *The Claw* (a reference to the apparent villain's artificial arm) hoping to attract an American investor, but no luck!

I was living in America when Michael Carreras reminded me of *The Claw*. He was back at Hammer now, full time. And very grateful we all were to see him. It wasn't until much later that I discovered he was having serious problems hanging onto the company that his father, Sir James, had tried to sell from right under his nose. Michael had personally borrowed the money to buy the company and now he was going to have to make a go of it. A sink or swim scenario. For a blow-by-blow description of what went on backstage, Denis Meikle's book, *A History of Horrors*, is an absolute must. There was more horror going on backstage than in front of the cameras.

In 1969 Michael dug out my old script, read it, then sent it to me to see if I could brighten it up somehow. I re-read it and decided the reason they hadn't made it earlier was because it wasn't good enough. And, at that time, I had no ideas for making it better. So I gave it to a writer friend of mine, Michael Syson, to see if maybe he could inject some juice into it. *The Claw* had been set on a houseboat moored near a big house, which I suggested could be Oakley Court. I must have been feeling nostalgic. Michael Syson came up with the idea of transferring the story to a cottage and a nearby boarding school. This was all that was needed. He did a quick rewrite and I gave it back to Michael Carreras, who decided that at last it was worth making.

The story was, as usual, a little convoluted and, I'm sure, familiar. Peggy Heller (Judy Geeson), recently recovered from a nervous breakdown, is preparing to meet her husband Robert (Ralph Bates) when she is attacked at her home by a one-armed man. Nobody believes her and she leaves to join Robert, who has just taken a job as teacher at a boys' boarding school,

Left: Michael Carmichael (Peter Cushing), the one-armed headmaster incriminated in **Fear in the Night** *(1972).*
Above: Robert Heller (Ralph Bates) tries to reassure his traumatised young wife Peggy (Judy Geeson) in **Fear in the Night** *(1972).*

Camera operator Neil Binney films the attack on Peggy (Judy Geeson) in **Fear in the Night** (1972).

goes to to Molly, who we now realise is Robert's lover, the two of them having primed Peggy to kill the unwanted Michael. Girl being driven mad again. I said it was familiar.

Anyway, Peggy remains catatonic so the lovers plan to force the truth from her and then fake her suicide by hanging. But Michael has been one step ahead of them. The gun with which Peggy shot him was loaded with blanks. Now there is a denouement scene during which Robert accidentally kills Molly. He is dragged away by Michael and hanged. As the police arrive, Peggy is wandering off down the driveway, crazier than she was at the beginning of the movie.

One of the reasons Michael decided to go ahead with the movie was because he wanted to make a double-bill called 'Women in Terror'. One of the pictures was called *Straight On Till Morning*, to be directed by Peter Collinson, so let's call the other *Fear in the Night*. He also asked me to produce and direct it. Why he did that after the last fiasco, I don't know. Maybe he too realised that *Lust for a Vampire* wasn't entirely my fault.

We cast pretty strongly with Ralph Bates in the lead. We persuaded Peter Cushing to come back to work. A sad man now, who never fully recovered from the death of his wife. Not that it affected his perform-

which at the moment is empty for the summer holidays. With the job has come a cottage in the school grounds. Peggy meets the headmaster of the school, Michael Carmichael (Peter Cushing), and later his wife Molly (Joan Collins).

Robert is forced to go to London on school business and that night Peggy is attacked again, once more by a one-armed man. Later, she realises that Michael Carmichael only has one arm, so he must be the man who is attacking her. While Robert is still away Michael comes over to the cottage and Peggy shoots him with a shotgun that Robert has left lying around. When Robert returns, Peggy is practically catatonic and is unable to tell him what has happened. Robert

EMI Anglo EMI Film Distributors Ltd. present
A HAMMER PRODUCTION
"**FEAR IN THE NIGHT**"
starring **Judy Geeson · Joan Collins**
Ralph Bates and **Peter Cushing** as the Headmaster
Screenplay by **JIMMY SANGSTER & MICHAEL SYSON**
Produced and Directed by **JIMMY SANGSTER**
TECHNICOLOR®   Distributed by Anglo EMI Film Distributors Ltd.

Ralph Bates receives the support of his director during a break in filming **Fear in the Night** (1972).

CLASSIC SCENE

FEAR IN THE NIGHT

I suppose the best scene in the movie is the one that takes place in the hall of the school just after the Joan Collins character has disappeared and Ralph Bates drags Judy Geeson in and starts having a conversation with the invisible Peter Cushing. He breaks up a great deal of furniture and ends up shooting Joan Collins by mistake, which, while not exactly a surprise, is nevertheless is a good moment.

 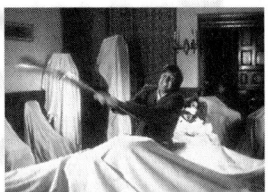  

ance in any way. He was still gentle and considerate and as sharp as a razor when he needed to be. As the female lead we cast Judy Geeson who had starred in *10 Rillington Place* and, as the heavy, Joan Collins. This was her pre-American soap days and she hadn't worked for some time. This was just as well because we'd never have got her for the money we were able to offer. She made a great villainess. Very beautiful and a great performance.

Unfortunately she wasn't an easy lady on the set. That could have been because she was pregnant at the time, a fact she'd omitted to mention when we were casting. The first time we knew about it was when the wardrobe mistress came to me and said that none of the clothes she'd bought for Joan a couple of weeks before production fitted her any longer and please would I tell her to stop eating so much. I mentioned it to Joan who told me she was pregnant and what the hell was I going to do about it. As with her general behaviour throughout the shooting, she managed to give the impression she was doing us all a big favour being in our picture. I suppose, in retrospect, she was.

The shooting was pretty straightforward. As usual Ralph Bates and I had a lot of fun which, again in retrospect, probably wasn't good for the picture. There are directors who deliberately create tension on a set because they feel that by getting people worked up they will give a better performance. All I know is that on *Lust for a Vampire* there was so much tension I dreaded coming to work every day. If it had produced good performances, it would have been okay, but it didn't. But then on *Fear in the Night*, which *was* fun, the performances weren't very good either.

But having said that, *Fear in the Night* was an okay movie. Some people liked it a lot. As it happens, I'm not one of them. But that's not because I think it was a bad script badly shot. I think it's because I became disenchanted with this type of subject. I'm not a great fan of any of the movies I directed. *The Horror of Frankenstein* and *Fear in the Night* just missed, *Lust for a Vampire* was a mile off. All, I feel, would have been better had they been directed by Terry Fisher. The only memorable thing about *Fear in the Night* was that it was the last movie I made for Hammer. It was 30 years ago.

THE CLAW

My copy of the The Claw is dated June 1967, and is very close to what I eventually shot as Fear in the Night over four years later. The characters in The Claw were subtly different from their counterparts in Fear in the Night, however. Michael and Molly Carmichael (played by Peter Cushing and Joan Collins in the movie) are Michael and Molly Castlemaine. Michael still has an artificial arm, but he is an estate manager, not a headmaster, in this version.

The major difference is the location. If you're familiar with the title sequence of Fear in the Night, the opening sequence of The Claw should illustrate how it was basically the same movie in a waterlogged setting:

EXT. RIVER BANK. NIGHT

The first and overwhelming impression that we get is of the rain.

We are on a river bank, shooting across the river. On the far side, moored permanently, is a large houseboat. But between us and the houseboat, is the rain. It is almost solid; it drums on the roof of the houseboat; it breaks up the surface of the river into a million tiny fountains; and the sound it makes is fierce and relentless.

There is one light burning in the houseboat, and even from here, we can make out the vague, shadowy silhouette of somebody standing in the window, looking out.

Over this we bring in our distributor's credit.

Then with the aid of a ZOOM, we start to move slowly towards the figure in the window, we DISSOLVE through to cover the major part of the track across, so that we are six feet from the window, and we recognise the figure as that of a woman.

But the face behind the glass is smeared with the rain that runs down the window. The features are impossible to pick out. There is something weird in the effect that the flowing water has on the face behind the glass, almost as though it was the face itself that was fluid,

The scheming Molly Carmichael (Joan Collins) in **Fear in the Night** (1972).

the features running down upon themselves, constantly shifting.

And on this shifting mirage of a face we bring in suddenly a gigantic clap of thunder, designed to lift the audience out of their seats.

And with this sound effect we bring in our Main Title.

We continue to move in towards the face after the main title.

Then the face moves behind the moving screen of the glass.

It presses up close to the glass, looking out sideways, trying to see something a little way down river.

LONG SHOT

From the deck of the houseboat, shooting along the side of the boat so as we know where we are.

Twenty feet down from the houseboat, a tree overhangs the river, its longest branches actually trailing in the water.

It is here that we first notice how fast the stream is running, visible in the V shaped breaks in the flow as it splits around a branch.

We see too, the body.

Fallen from the houseboat, the body has been carried the twenty feet downstream where it has become caught in one of the branches from the tree.

The pressure of the water has managed to lift it slightly up onto the branch, so that the head and shoulders are clear of the water, held outstretched by the pressure of the current.

We do not see the face, but just sufficient of the body to recognise it as that of a man.

CHAPTER 20

The Ones That Got Away

This chapter deals with the movies I was involved in which, for one reason or another, didn't get made. A couple went as far as a full shooting script. The first of these was during Hammer's 'tits and swords' period, when I wrote an original script for Michael Carreras first called *Midnight Jones*, later changed to *The Bride of Newgate Gaol*.

Hammer had wanted a restoration comedy to cash in on the success of movies like *Tom Jones* and *Moll Flanders*. Unfortunately, by the time they got around to making a decision, that kind of picture was no longer very popular, so they shelved it. It emerged later as part of an announced group of movies that Hammer was going to make in 1969, retitled *The Reluctant Virgin*. Still it didn't make it.

This was a pity because it was a fun script to write and I feel it would have made a good movie. Along with the regular storyline, which I can't even begin to remember, I had a running character, a singing minstrel, who would pop up every now and then, strum his lute, and sing to us, the audience, what was happening behind the scenes. This is how the script opened:

MIDNIGHT JONES

FADE IN:
EXT. GRAVEYARD. NIGHT.
A slow pan around the graveyard until we see the BALLADEER who is sitting cross-legged on one of the tombstones. Now he glances into CAMERA, puts down the sandwich he was eating and takes up his mandolin. A couple of

experimental strums before he looks back into CAMERA and starts to sing.

BALLADEER:
  I'll sing a ballad, tell a tale,
  of love and lust and hate,
  All occurring, year of grace,
  Seventeen ninety eight.

He nods out of frame.

BALLADEER:
  Over yonder dwells a lad,
  An orphan all his life,
  At this moment, aged nineteen,
  About to take a wife.

INT. CAPABILITY JONES' SHACK. NIGHT.
PEGGY is on the bed, her arms upraised towards CAPABILITY who is ruefully undoing his trousers.

BALLADEER:
  But why is he so slow to start,
  Why the worried frown?
  'Tis because the wife he beds,
  Belongs to Blacksmith Brown.

As Capability steps out of his trousers, Peggy grabs him, pulling him down on top of her.

Hollywood star Vincent Price was set to star as the sinister Molesworth in **The Fairytale Man**.

EXT. GRAVEYARD. NIGHT.
BLACKSMITH BROWN, a huge man, is creeping through towards Capability's shack. We pan with him. As he enters the shack, the balladeer continues.

BALLADEER:
  See the blacksmith, mighty man

Over, we HEAR a roar of rage.

  Hear his angry roar,
  It bodes no good for our poor lad,
  But it's happened all before.

INT. CAPABILITY'S. NIGHT.
Peggy is sitting up on the bed clutching a blanket to her nude figure. The Blacksmith is dodging round the bed trying to catch Capability who is wearing just his shirt. The Blacksmith has a large knife in his hand.

BLACKSMITH: I told you... next time I
  caught you and my wife at it I'd cut 'em off.

Capability manages to duck past the Blacksmith and out of the door.

EXT. GRAVEYARD. NIGHT.
Capability runs across the graveyard and ducks behind a gravestone as the Blacksmith appears at the door of the hut with Peggy hanging onto his arm.

PEGGY: Please Ben... leave him... he meant
  no harm.
BLACKSMITH: I'll skin him alive... so help
  me.
PEGGY: He don't know what he's doin'...
  he's a bit simple... honest... please Ben...
  come on, let's go home.

She whispers something in his ear. He looks a little mollified and then she whispers something else, putting her arms around him seductively. The Blacksmith gives in. He starts to walk off

with Peggy. Then he turns and shouts to the seemingly empty graveyard.

BLACKSMITH (shouting): You hear me,
  Capability Jones... next time I'll cut 'em off
  for sure.

Peggy pulls at his arm.

  ...all right, woman. I'm coming, I'm
  coming. What was that you said you was
  going to do for me?

He and Peggy move off around the corner of the church.

ANGLE
Capability straightens up from behind a tombstone in foreground, looking heartily relieved. He starts to walk back to his hut. As he does so, he passes the Balladeer.

BALLADEER:
  Capability Jones his name,
  Of that you're now aware,
  His is the tale of which I tell,
  and which you all will share.

This sequence is followed straight on with another seduction scene, this one with the vicar's wife who now breaks into his shack.
  Over the balladeer continues his tale.

BALLADEER:
  He spends his days... and nights as well
  In fear of life and limb.
  Because the women of the town
  Can't keep their hands off him.

  And here it starts, with our poor boy,
  All aching limbs and bones,
  The story of a sexy lad,
  The tale of Midnight Jones.

We bring in the MAIN TITLE over this.....

...and the movie starts. Silly perhaps, but a lot of fun to write. Pity it wasn't made.

In 1970 I wrote a treatment based on John Blackburn's novel *Bury Him Darkly*. Hammer even commissioned poster artwork for that one, but prospective producer Tony Nelson Keys couldn't find any takers. Another one that got away was called *The Big Wheel*. Actually, on reflection, I'm not all that surprised. It was a story about big business and the wheeling and dealing power struggles that go on at the top of a big corporation. Why I ever wrote it I can't imagine and why Hammer were interested is even more perplexing. Anyway, they didn't make it.

Next was *The Fairytale Man*. If anyone asked me what I consider the top three scripts I ever wrote, I'd have to include this one.

'*The Fairytale Man*? Never heard of it!' I can hear everyone saying. A reasonable reaction because it was never made. At least, it *was* made but with a different title, not by Hammer, and only after rewrites to the extent that the final screen credits ran *Screenplay by Mary Rodgers, based on a story by Mary Rodgers and Jimmy Sangster*. Okay! I admit we both based our idea on the *Faust* legend. But then so have dozens of others – books, operas, plays, you name it. All of them have used the 'selling one's soul to the devil' storyline. My only consolation in the affair (apart from the money) was the fact that I got to share a screen credit with the daughter of Richard Rodgers... that's the Richard Rodgers who wrote all the great musicals. Would that his daughter had been as good a screenwriter as her father was a musician.

In my opinion, it was thanks mainly to the rewrites that Disney managed to make an indifferent movie out of the story, starring Elliott Gould and Bill Cosby, which they called *The Devil and Max Devlin*. Let me quote to you from a review by Geoff Brown in *Time Out* magazine. 'The film finally subsides in a welter of structural flaws and heartwarming sentiment.' I honestly think if they'd stuck to my original script they would have had a really good movie. But then I'm biased.

But this is supposed to be a book about Hammer, so why am I bothering to write about it? Two reasons. One, it was designed for Hammer, they were involved from the start. And two, maybe there are enough of you out there who will be interested in all the to-ing and fro-ing that goes on *before* a movie ever gets onto the floor.

It was 1973. I was already in America when the whole thing started. I had a partner over there, Harold Cohen, with whom I'd turned my first two novels, *private i* and *Foreign Exchange,* into Movies of the Week for the ABC network. I mentioned to Harold that maybe, if I could come up with a subject, he and Hammer could get together and co-produce it. He liked the idea, so I called Michael Carreras, who was managing director of Hammer by then, and put the idea to him.

'Fine,' he said. 'Providing we can attract a name.'

I was living in Beverly Hills at the time. Across the street from me lived Vincent Price. 'Would he do?' I asked.

Michael agreed he would so I set out to write the script with Vincent Price firmly in mind. The fact that when the film was eventually made Bill Cosby played the part just shows how different the two concepts were.

It was a pretty straightforward idea. An old devil named Molesworth (Vincent Price) needs to get some people to sign away their souls. He's a long dead Victorian actor, a rather incompetent, lower grade demon who, if he doesn't get some souls pretty damn quick, is going to be demoted, a fact made very clear to him by his business-suited, executive-type Chief Demon.

Molesworth gets summoned up to Earth by three children who proceed to make an absolute idiot of him as he transports them to various historic/fairytale situations. In them, he puts the children in predicaments of dire peril, hoping they'll sign the contracts in order to escape from the dreadful fate confronting them. They become aristocratic children in the French Revolution; they are taken by Blackbeard the pirate; they come within an inch of being eaten in the Gingerbread House; finally they are threatened by Dracula... Only then do they eventually sign away their souls to escape. Back in Hell, Molesworth presents the contracts to his superior, who congratulates him and offers to show him what will eventually happen to the children. Molesworth is so horrified by the sight of eternal hellfire and brimstone that he steals the contracts back and delivers them to the children.

A couple of scenes from my original script, dated 1973, will show you the style of the movie I wanted to make. We have these three children, Mary aged ten, John aged nine and Jenny aged six. Jenny, unbeknown to anyone, has psychic powers, and while playing around with their uncle's Ouija board makes a contact.

INT. CELL. NIGHT.
A small, monastic-like cubicle, one stone slab for a bed, nothing else. And on the slab, suddenly, sitting into a startled CLOSE SHOT, CHARLES W MOLESWORTH.

MOLESWORTH: Huh... what... ?

He looks round the cell. Nobody there. He starts to lay back on the slab once more.

JENNY *(voice over)*: Hey! Wake up!

He sits up again, realises what is happening and with a long-suffering look, he puts his feet to the floor.

MOLESWORTH: Oh heaven! (as opposed to 'Oh hell')

INT. NURSERY. NIGHT.
The three children, gathered around the Ouija board. Jenny looks at the other two.

JENNY: He's awake. What shall I ask him?
JOHN: Ask him... oh, you're making it up. I'm going to bed.

Jenny doesn't care one little bit. She starts to turn away from the board.

JENNY: OK...
MARY: Ask him... ask him something nobody knows.
JENNY: That's silly.
MARY: No it's not... that'll prove it. Ask him what I'm going to buy Mummy for her birthday. Only I know that. I haven't told anyone.

JENNY: OK. Hey... what's Mary buying Mummy for her birthday?
INT. CELL. NIGHT.
Molesworth, sitting on the edge of his bed.

MOLESWORTH: To be awakened from my slumbers for such trivialities...

He concentrates, nevertheless.

INT. NURSERY. NIGHT.
Jenny's hand on the Ouija board starts spelling it out. Mary reads it.

MARY: p...e...r...f...u...m...e. Perfume.

Jenny looks disappointed.

JENNY: That's the same as scent, isn't it. I was going to buy her scent.
MARY: I only decided today... he *knew*.
JOHN: All right... you're so clever... let's see what he looks like.
JENNY: Who?
JOHN: *Him.*
MARY: Can you do that?
JENNY: I dunno. I can try. Hey... !

INT. CELL NIGHT.
Molesworth, who was about to relax back on his slab bed, sits up again.

JENNY *(voice over)*: We want to see you.

Molesworth groans.

MOLESWORTH: Oh no...
JENNY *(voice over... louder)*: We want to see you.

Molesworth puts a finger to his lips.

MOLESWORTH: Please... keep your voice low.
JENNY *(voice over... much louder)*: Can't you hear me... ?

MOLESWORTH *(muttering)*: I shall have to get a pass. *(looks up towards the ceiling)* No!

INT. NURSERY. NIGHT.
Jenny's hand on the Ouija board.

MARY: n...o... no.
JOHN: See! I told you.
MARY: Order him to.
JENNY: OK. I order you to come here.
MARY: Say 'command'. It sounds better.
JENNY: I command you...

IN. CELL. NIGHT.
Molesworth, where we left him. Over, we hear the last word of Jenny as it starts to echo and reverberate.

JENNY *(voice over)*: ... command... command... command...

An alarm bell starts to ring nearby.

MOLESWORTH: That's done it.

He reaches under his straw-filled pillow and pulls out a small, dog-eared instruction booklet. He leafs through the pages, looking for something.

MOLESWORTH: Command appearance... command appearance... here we are. *(reading)* 'When an appearance is specifically commanded, the alarm signal will sound. At that time the following procedure must be followed. One, stop time at the source of the command.

He looks towards the ceiling and snaps his fingers.

INT. NURSERY. NIGHT.
The children are frozen into immobility. Even the dog, who has crept in to see what's going on, is frozen in his tracks.

INT. CELL. NIGHT.
Molesworth looks back at the manual.

Vincent Price in **Percy's Progress** (1974), *a film made in the UK around the time Hammer wanted him for Jimmy's* **The Fairytale Man**.

MOLESWORTH *(reading)*: 'Two. Report to immediate superior.

He closes the book and gets to his feet wearily.

MOLESWORTH: Oh that this too, too solid flesh would melt, thaw and resolve itself into a dew. *Hamlet*. Act One. Scene Two.

He reaches for his clothes.

INT. CORRIDOR. HELL. NIGHT.
Molesworth, wearing a black suit (circa 1840) complete with cape, comes along the corridor. There are a few people in the corridor. They are dressed in a variety of costumes dating all through the spectrum of history, up to the present day. Nobody takes any notice of anybody else. Molesworth reaches a bank of elevators and presses a button. Then he stands waiting. As he waits he is joined by a young, sharp-looking guy, Madison Avenue dressed, who shoots his cuffs and adjusts his necktie as he stands there. They stand side by side without talking, waiting for the elevator. The young guy's name is BARNABY. Finally...

BARNABY: Hello Molesworth.
MOLESWORTH: Mr Barnaby.

BARNABY: Command appearance?
MOLESWORTH: Right.
BARNABY: Don't see you around much. How long since you've been up?

A moment's pause, then Molesworth mumbles something unintelligible.

BARNABY: Sorry. Didn't hear you.
MOLESWORTH: Eighty-two years.

Barnaby looks at him aghast. At that moment the elevator arrives. The doors open. The Elevator Operator is a uniformed young devil with a long tail, which he keeps neatly folded over his arm.

OPERATOR: Where to, fellas?
MOLESWORTH: Executive level please.
BARNABY: Me too.
OPERATOR: Going down.

EXECUTIVE LEVEL. HELL. NIGHT.
This is a large room with secretaries sitting outside of their various offices working on their computers. All of them are luscious-looking females. Molesworth and Barnaby come out of the elevator. Barnaby moves off while Molesworth approaches one of the secretaries. She ignores him. He clears his throat. Finally she looks up.

SECRETARY: Yes?
MOLESWORTH: I've had a command appearance.
SECRETARY: Name?
MOLESWORTH: Molesworth... Charles W... Thespian.

She looks up at him.

MOLESWORTH: Actor.

The secretary announces him on her intercom.

VOICE: Send him in.

Molesworth goes through to the inner office.

INT. OFFICE. HELL. NIGHT.
A large, sterile, functional office, all chrome and leather. Behind the desk, a business-suited executive, GREELEY. He's tapping away on his computer.

GREELEY *(without looking up)*: Come in, Molesworth.

Finally he looks up from the screen.

GREELEY: Eighty-two years... ?
MOLESWORTH: I fear so, Mr Greeley.
GREELEY: Your file comes up for review soon. You haven't brought us a good healthy soul for... (looks at the screen) ... you've never brought us a soul.

The scene goes on for a little longer wherein Molesworth is warned that if he doesn't get a soul or two, he's going to be in severe trouble. He leaves the office and goes back to the elevator where he tells the operator to go 'all the way up'. And we cut to the nursery.

INT. NURSERY. NIGHT.
The children are still frozen in their previous attitudes, then, movement.

MARY: Say it again.
JENNY: I command you.
JOHN: Oh come on... let's go to bed...

He heads for the door and then he stops suddenly. The three of them all stare into the far corner of the room while the dog lets out a whine of fear and shoots under the table. The door that leads to the toy cupboard crashes open... a cloud of smoke, and there is Molesworth.

OPERATOR *(voice off)*: Top floor. Watch your step.

The door to the toy cupboard slams shut. Molesworth throws his cape around him with a grand gesture, surveying the room. He intones sonorously.

MOLESWORTH: From the bottomless pit; from beyond the great divide; from the eternal nethermost reaches of the universe... I submit to your command.

Then he becomes aware that he is being stared at by three wide-eyed kids and a dog.

MOLESWORTH: Sorry. I seem to have miscalculated.

He looks into the toy cupboard. That's all it is, a toy cupboard. Back to the children.

MOLESWORTH (cont'd): Are there any... any adults in this house?

The children tell him that they are the ones who commanded him up and he gets reasonably excited at the chance of capturing three souls in one fell swoop. But when he offers the children whatever their hearts desire in exchange for a signature on a contract, none of them can think of anything and they decide they've had enough of Molesworth and 'Thank you very much, but we're going to bed now.' Molesworth panics and freezes time again while he pulls out his instruction booklet once more.

MOLESWORTH (reading to himself): In the unlikely event that you encounter a subject with no apparent unfulfilled desires, it is suggested that the subject is placed in an untenable position whereby his or her only recourse is to seek your aid. As in all cases, it is vital that you obtain the signature before you come to his or her aid.

So he sets out to offer to take the children to various romantic places where he intends that things go horribly wrong so that he can get their signatures. He shows them a pirate book in the nursery featuring Blackbeard. That sounds fun to the kids, so they are transported there. Molesworth connives to get them sentenced to walk the plank, but somehow they get out of it.

Next they become children of the French Revolution. Again they handle everything on their own. This being a Hammer film, there is a Dracula/Frankenstein sequence which nearly does the trick for Molesworth. But it is the Gingerbread House sequence where he is able to get their signatures as an alternative to being eaten by the witch. The children are returned safely home, while Molesworth descends once more to Hell and a meeting with Greeley.

INT. GREELEY'S OFFICE. NIGHT.
The three contracts are spread out on Greeley's desk. Molesworth stands opposite him. Greeley looks up from the contracts.

GREELEY: Admirable Mr Molesworth... three contracts all signed and sealed. It will look good on your record, which, if you don't mind me saying, hasn't been exactly exemplary up to now.
MOLESWORTH: Thank you, Mr Greeley.
GREELEY: Yes... admirable. Its always gratifying to capture souls so young... untarnished... innocent... untouched by the harsh realities of life up there.

Molesworth starts to look uncomfortable.

MOLESWORTH: Yes sir.
GREELEY: Three shiny new souls... oh Molesworth, if only those foolish mortals realised what they were doing. To exchange a moment of time for an eternity of damnation. They're idiots, all of them.
MOLESWORTH: Mr Greeley, sir... I've never really seen where we send the damned souls. What's it like?
GREELEY: Come... I'll show you.

He gets to his feet and we see, for the first time, that he has a long tail, which he now tucks neatly over his arm He starts for the door.

GREELEY: Everyone down here should see what results from a signature on a contract. It provides a constant spur to initiative.

They both go out.

INT. EXECUTIVE LEVEL. HELL. NIGHT.
Greeley and Molesworth come from the office and move down the passage to where there is an observation window. Half a dozen people are standing outside the window looking through... and down. They are enjoying what they see. Someone sees Greeley and nudges his companion and room is made for Greeley and Molesworth to move through to the front. They both look down through the observation window.

GREELEY: There you are, Molesworth. Hell and eternal damnation.

CLOSE. MOLESWORTH
Reflected on his face is flickering fire as he looks down through the glass. His expression becomes one of absolute horror.

ANGLE – WIDER
Greeley speaks without looking up from the window.

GREELEY: Every operator should see the end results of his work... keeps you on your toes...

He digs Molesworth with his elbow.

GREELEY: ... eh, Molesworth?

Molesworth gulps.

GREELEY: Turn up the sound, someone.

A man turns up a volume switch. From a speaker above the window comes the sounds of hell and damnation... the cries of lost souls, their torment and their agony... the crack of whips... the gurgling of the swamp... the snarls

of carnivores... the whole cacophony of hell. Molesworth looks sick as the others laugh among themselves.

MOLESWORTH: That's where the children will be going... ?

GREELEY: The children? Oh yes... the children... *your* children. Yes, Molesworth, that's where they'll be going. Thanks to your good work.

MOLESWORTH: Excuse me a moment.

He backs out of the group around the window and moves off.

ANGLE
Greeley's secretary looks up as Molesworth comes into shot.

MOLESWORTH: Mr Greeley forgot his glasses. He asked me to fetch them for him.

The secretary, bored, nods towards the office. Molesworth goes in.

INT. GREELEY'S OFICE.
Molesworth comes in. He closes the door behind him, walks over to the desk and gathers up the three contracts where Greeley left them. Folding them and putting them in his pocket, he walks out again.

INT. EXECUTIVE LEVEL. HELL.
Molesworth comes out and over to the elevator. He presses the button and a moment later, the doors open.

ELEVATOR GUY: Where to, friend?
MOLESWORTH: Up.
ELEVATOR GUY: All the way?
MOLESWORTH: All the way.

He steps in and the doors slide shut.

INT. LIVING ROOM. DAY.
The children's house. A birthday party in progress. Among the guests we recognise John, Mary and Jenny (whose birthday it is). Kate (mother) is talking to Nanny.

KATE: Has the cake arrived yet?
NANNY: Yes ma'am. The caterer just brought it in. He's in the kitchen.
KATE: Oh good!

She heads off towards the kitchen. CAMERA PANS with her and then settles on a group of children. Jenny is opening her gifts. Sitting close to her, along with a couple of the other guests, are John and Mary. She produces a doll from a parcel... oohs and aahs and she takes the next present, an envelope.

JOHN: Bet it's money.

She opens it... pulls out folded paper, unfolds the paper and we recognise the three contracts. She looks up at John and Mary. Then they look out as Kate calls.

KATE *(off)*: Everyone... the cake... !

ANGLE
The kitchen door; the cake, held high by a waiter, emerges from the kitchen. On the cake, seven candles, all alight. The waiter carries the cake across to Jenny and then lowers it to her level so that she can blow out the candles. She does so, and is left face to face with the waiter, Charles W Molesworth. A moment's pause and he gives her a broad wink.

FADE OUT

THE END

And that was it. Not a regular Hammer movie by any means. But at that time, Hammer were trying to expand beyond the Gothics, and they considered they might get somewhere with a kids' movie.

And maybe they would have, but we'll never know.

Michael Carreras had his people do a schedule and a budget. A six-week shooting schedule and a budget of £280,000. At the $2.50 rate of exchange at that time, it came to $700,000. That included $75,000 for Vincent Price and the princely sum of $12,500 for the script. I know things were a lot cheaper in those days but, even so, it was not an expensive movie to make. Nevertheless, Michael was unable to raise the necessary finance and the whole project went on hold. A couple of years later, I dug it out of my bottom drawer and sent it to Disney. They liked it, so I bought it back from Michael and sold it to them. They then proceeded to really screw it up. *The Devil and Max Devlin* was the result. It was so completely different to my script that I wonder they bothered paying me at all. But they did and, as I said before, I ended up with half a 'from a story by' credit.

I don't think many people saw the movie, which isn't surprising. It got bad reveiws, and while Elliott Gould and Bill Cosby had reasonably high-profile names, Cosby was nowhere near the huge star he became later. Gould played the part of a sleazy guy who is killed and goes to Hell. There he is told by a devil (played by Bill Cosby) that his life here in Hell will be much easier if he manages to get some souls signed away. He is given three individuals to get signatures from: a girl who wants to be a pop singer, a young student guy who wants to be a motor cross star and a young boy of around ten years old. So up he goes, with Bill Cosby appearing occasionally to give him advice. He has the power to make the girl sing and become a star, the young guy to become a successful motor cross rider and he even cons the young kid by being Mr Nice Guy and offering to marry the kid's widowed mother – so that he, Gould, will become the kid's father. He succeeds in all these endeavours but, at the last minute, he reneges on the deal because he's started to like his victims and he's rescued by heavenly intervention. Suddenly he's not dead any longer.

It was on TV recently. In a potted review it was described as 'preposterous rubbish'.

Okay! Maybe my movie with Vincent Price would have turned out to be preposterous rubbish too. But I don't think so, and it's something we're never going to find out.

EPILOGUE

So, that was me and Hammer, on a picture-to-picture basis. Around 25 years of my working life, up to age 45 or thereabouts. There were other movies for other people, lots of them, both during the latter part of those 25 years and before. In my late teens there was Carlton Hill Studios, Ealing Studios... culminating when I was dragged off screaming to a couple of years in India by the RAF. Not, I hasten to say, because I'd anything against India, but for me, already three years into my career, it seemed such a terrible waste of time. Then, finally, there was another lifetime in America.

My first staff job in America was directly due to Hammer, inasmuch as Columbia wanted to make a TV series entitled *Ghost Story*. Twenty-two hour-long episodes. The show was to be produced by Bill Castle, the king of American schlock horror movies at that time. He had shot a picture for Hammer at Bray in 1962. *The Old Dark House*. I'd got to know him then. Added to this, the business affairs manager of Screen Gems, Columbia's TV division, was Seymour Friedman who had directed one of the early Hammer films on which I had been his assistant director. These two got their heads together and my name came up as a possible story consultant. This is the term they use to describe a script editor in Hollywood. They called Tony Hinds at Hammer to ask if they could borrow me and Tony told them I hadn't been around for years. So they called my agent who called me and asked if I wanted the job.

'What's a story consultant?' I wanted to know.

He told me.

'Does it pay well?' I asked.

It did, and I took the job.

By the time the series had finished, I was a permanent fixture in LA, with a new wife (since gone) and a large house in Beverly Hills, complete with mortgage.

During the next 15 years or thereabouts I wrote three or four theatrical movies (one for John Huston, would you believe?) and half a dozen movies for TV, one of which starred Christopher Lee, another, Bette Davis. I also wrote over 100 hours of American prime time TV and I produced an ill-fated TV series for CBS about Dan'l Boone.

Somewhere during that period I wrote eight novels, two of which I filmed. Basically I suppose one could say that after I left Hammer the good times continued to roll. They certainly paid better.

I had a good time working for the old firm even if I didn't make much money. Here's an interesting fact. I had a profit sharing percentage (ten per cent of the producers' profits) on ten of the movies I made for Hammer. Even now, 25 five years after it all happened, I have never seen a single penny. Does that mean the company never made a profit on any of those movies? If it does, it's no wonder they packed it in. Trouble is, the company has changed hands so many times in the past few years it's not possible to find out any more.

In my opinion, Hammer is a ship that lost its rudder a long time ago. Since then it has been wallowing around under very little control while various people and/or corporations try to get it back on course. Or, rather, they talk about getting it back on course without actually knowing the course they want it on. A lot of talk from a lot of people, and nothing happens. The only people keeping Hammer alive are the fans.

Problem is, as I see it, the Hammer era has gone. And by the Hammer era, I mean the Gothics, the movies that made the company what it was. And they just aren't popular any more. Other people have tried making them – Kenneth Branagh's Frankenstein, Stephen Frears' Jekyll and Hyde – spending on one picture nearly as much money as Hammer spent during its entire existence. None of them have been box office hits, with the freak exception of Coppola's Dracula. As for the 'psycho' cycle that I started at Hammer, that's still going, but it was already going long before Hammer moved in that direction.

But I still look back on my Hammer years with fond memories. There are the friends, both those who are still around, like Tony Hinds and Freddie Francis, and those who aren't, like Michael Carreras and Ralph Bates. And, let's face it, it is because of Hammer that I've had such a good life. I mean, at my age, who could want more? A nice house; a perfect wife, former actress Mary Peach, whom I love very much; a whole bunch of children and grandchildren; some money in the bank. Not much, but enough. Let's face it: Heaven!

And I guess that's about it. I hope you've enjoyed reading this book as much as I enjoyed writing it.

INDEX

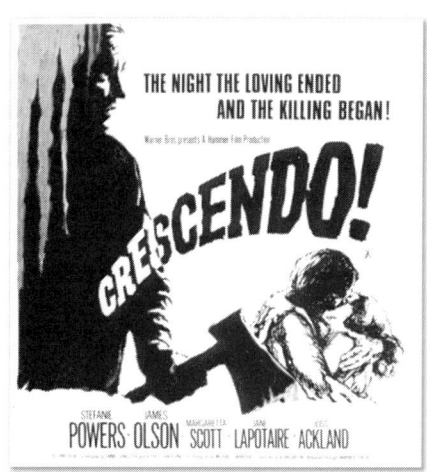

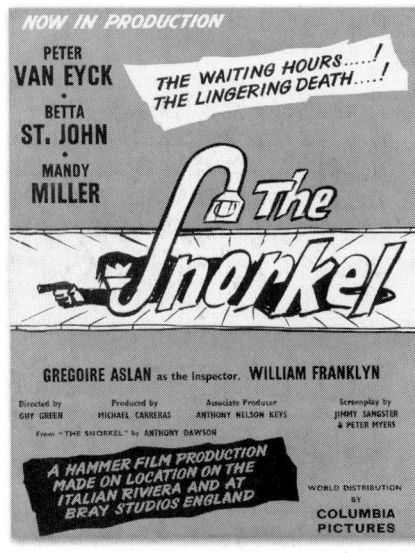